D0854841

BIG U

Also by I. G. Edmonds:

Micronesia
Pakistan
Automotive Tuneups for Beginners
Ethiopia
Magic Makers: A History of Magic

BIG U

Universal in the Silent Days

I. G. Edmonds

SOUTH BRUNSWICK AND NEW YORK: A.S. BARNES AND COMPANY
LONDON: THOMAS YOSELOFF LTD

A. S. Barnes and Co., Inc.
Cranbury, New Jersey 08512

Thomas Yoseloff Ltd
Magdalen House
136-148 Tooley Street
London SE1 2TT, England

Library of Congress Cataloging in Publication Data

Edmonds, I   G
   Big U: Universal in the silent days.

   Includes indexes.
   1. Universal Film Manufacturing Company. I. Title.
PN1999.U58E3 1977   791.43'09794'94   76-10874
ISBN 0-498-01809-1

to

OLIVER DERNBERGER
I am but one of many historians,
collectors, and movie buffs who are indebted to
Oliver for the generous way he shares his vast
knowledge of studios, films, and film folk.

Printed in the United States of America

Contents

Photographic Acknowledgments

The following copyrighted photographs are used with the special permission of Universal City Studios:

The Fourflusher, copyright 1927-28 by Universal Pictures Corp.

Blake of Scotland Yard, copyright 1927 by Universal Pictures Corp.

Cat and the Canary, copyright 1927 by Universal Pictures Corp.

Uncle Tom's Cabin, copyright 1927 by Universal Pictures Corp.

A Cheerful Fraud, copyright 1927 by Universal Pictures Corp.

I am informed by the Universal City Studios legal department that the Universal film *Show Boat* copyright was sold to MGM.

Other photographs used were originally copyrighted by the Independent Motion Picture Company, The Universal Film Manufacturing Company, Bluebird Productions, Inc., L-KO Films, and the Universal Pictures Corp. between the years 1909 and 1929. I have carefully consulted copyright records and renewal records and believe these pictures to be in the public domain, no record of their copyright renewal having been found. Copyright renewal is a complicated legal subject and others expecting to use these same photographs are advised to make their own copyright search.

The photographs are from my collection, assembled over a period of forty years. It is not possible to thank all who have contributed to it, but special mention should be made of Milton Luboviski, Leonard Brown, Malcolm Willets, and above all, Oliver Dernberger and Kenneth G. Lawrence, both of whom went out of their way to be helpful.

Introduction

"We'll have to have a name. What'll we call the company?"

The speaker was "Pat" Powers, an ex-phonograph salesman turned movie distributor.

None of the other six men seated around the heavy oak table in the New York office of the Laemmle Film Service replied to Powers's question. Then a tiny man—five-foot-two in height—turned from the window where he had stepped to clear his nose of the heavy cigar smoke in the room. He had just seen a dray wagon pass in the street below. It had "Universal Piping Company" lettered on its side. The sign appealed to the little man.

"Gentlemen," Carl Laemmle said, resuming his seat at the conference table, "This merger will make us the biggest film manufacturing company in the universe. Why not call ourselves The Universal Film Company?"

There was no disagreement and the new conglomerate became "The Universal Film Manufacturing Company." Later an advertising slogan was tacked on to the corporate name: "The Largest Film Manufacturing Concern in the Universe."

Actually, the name "Film Manufacturing Company" was incorrect. Universal did not intend to make films. It was intended to be the distribution unit and banker for the individual producers who would continue to make their own films.

So began in June 1912 the company that became Universal Pictures, today the oldest and most active of the great studios that built the motion picture industry.

Movie historians do not devote a lot of space to Universal, except to record Carl Laemmle's bitter fight to break the motion picture trust. They like to dismiss Universal in the silent film era as a film factory lorded over by a lovable but eccentric old man who only hired his relatives.

Nothing could be further from the truth. When Universal was formed Carl Laemmle was in his prime as a businessman. He made Universal a true pioneering organization. It made such films as the sensational *Traffic in Souls.* Von Stroheim's *Blind Husbands,* Alan Holubar's *20,000 Leagues Under the Sea* with its remarkable undersea photography, Wallace Worsley's *Hunchback of Notre Dame* with Lon Chaney in his greatest role, Clarence Brown's *Goose Woman,* Sven Gade's *Siege,* Paul Leni's *The Cat and the Canary,* and others that any studio of their day would have been proud to present.

It is true that Carl Laemmle, during Big U's silent years, found jobs for his legion of relatives. But with a few notable exceptions they were put in jobs where they did not interfere with the business of turning out profitable films. Studio manager Isadore Bernstein okayed the budget and some of the stories. Director-general Henry McRae then okayed all the stories. Once story and budget were passed, the "producer" —actually the director and frequently the writer as well—was on his own. He was only required to make an entertaining film that made money.

Later there was front-office interference, but in the beginning Universal hired good directors and left them alone. Laemmle tried to look at most of the films made in Universal's first decade and would occasionally shelve one he thought below the company's standard.

The men who made Big U's films in the beginning were uncommonly efficient. All went on

Carl Laemmle was president of Universal Pictures from 1912 to 1936.

to work later for major studios. Among them were Tod Browning, Herbert Brenon, Frank Lloyd, Clarence Brown, Robert Z. Leonard, John Ford, Jack Conway, Allan Dwan, William A. Seiter, Charles Brabin, Edward Sloman, and Maurice Tourneur.

The star roster included people who reached their greatest fame at Universal like Pauline Bush, Dorothy Phillips, Mary Philbin, Priscilla Dean, Norman Kerry, Reginald Denny, and others. But not so well known is that many famous names

from other studios either got their apprenticeship at Universal or worked for Laemmle at one time or another. They include Mary Pickford, Jack Pickford, Hoot Gibson, Helen Holmes, Pearl White, Art Acord, Lewis Stone, Clive Brook, Mae Murray, Lois Wilson, Edward Everett Horton, Jean Hersholt, Wallace Beery, Sarah Bernhardt, Alma Rubens, Laura LaPlante, House Peters and (in 1928) Walt Disney with his Oswald the Lucky Rabbit.

From the beginning Laemmle promised distributors he would give them "quality products." The stories did not always live up to this promise, although they were as good as those made by other studios of the day. Photography-wise and in sets and costuming Big U did better than many companies. Until about 1920, Big U's stars competed with the entire industry. In 1914 J. Warren Kerrigan was considered the most popular male star in America.

The fact is that Universal was more than just a film factory. It was a major studio playing a major role in the development of the motion picture industry. The accomplishments of Universal and the talented people who made its pictures and sold them to the public make a long neglected story that deserves to be told.

This account is based upon interviews with many people over a long period of time, upon books, magazines, and yellowed newspapers. The facts given here, and sometimes the dates, vary from other accounts. Often a researcher can find absolutely opposing stories about some historical fact and then will meet an old actor who will give you still another account, along with the confidential information that it was he who taught D. W. Griffith all he knew. Far too much of what passes for motion picture history is legend and old stories invented or embellished by imaginative press agents. In such cases a writer must choose what his own research indicates is the correct account.

The silent films were make-believe. So is their history. I worked hard to make this account accurate. I do not presume to believe that I entirely succeeded.

1 The Birth of Universal

Memories fade with the years and egos balloon. So it is that the recollections of those who took part in historic events do not always agree with each other. The meeting in the office of the New York Motion Picture Company in February 1912 is an exception. Later, at different times, all the principals related essentially the same story.

Fred Balshofer, head of the company's production operations on the West Coast, came to New York to discuss urgent problems with his partners, Mr. Adam (Addie) Kessel and Mr. Charlie Bauman.

Balshofer was tall, blond, and wavy haired. He had an open, frank face and was known as a man whose word was as good as a written contract.

Addie Kessel was thin and dark haired. His stare was about as warm as a block of ice. He had been a bookie until the police put him out of business. His partner, Charlie Bauman, was short, pudgy, and wore the type of moustache later popularized by Groucho Marx. He appeared more jovial than Kessel, but since he had been associated with Addie in bookmaking, no one was fooled by his friendly appearance. Bauman, like Kessel, came up from a hard school.

Some years before this particular meeting one of Kessel's betting clients was unable to cover a wager he had placed with Addie. This man owned a film exchange. He bought short movie reels from producers and rented them out to small exhibitors whose business did not permit them to buy films outright. Addie, after asking for his $3,500 twice and not getting it, went down to the film exchange

and told the owner, "You are working for *me* now. I'm taking over this place."

There was no argument and Kessel brought in his friend Bauman to help with the business. Kessel intended to sell out as soon as possible, but changed his mind when he discovered how profitable a film exchange could be. They bought film for twelve cents a foot and rented it out to make several hundred percent profit. This profit grew as new theaters opened up.

Unfortunately, they soon discovered a snake in their movie Eden. This blight—in their view—was Thomas A. Edison, the noted inventor, who held United States patents on the motion picture camera and projector. Edison felt that anyone using either, without paying him a license, was stealing his property.

Edison launched a determined program to put all independent motion picture producers out of business. Kessel and Bauman found their sources of film disappearing as Edison closed first one and then another of the independents.

At this point the two ex-bookies decided to make their own films. They teamed with Fred Balshofer, who had been put out of business twice by Edison, and formed the New York Motion Picture Company. The company prospered from the beginning, but ran into difficulties while it operated at Fort Lee, New Jersey, because of harassment by goons hired by the Edison group. Balshofer moved production to California to escape from Edison's spies while Bauman and

Fred Balshofer and Charlie Bauman pose with members of
their New York Motion Picture Company in 1911. Buster
Edmonds and Bebe Daniels are the children between them.
Art Acord is at the top left.

Kessel remained in New York to market the film
Balshofer sent them.

In California Balshofer had the good fortune to
meet Col. Joe Miller, who with his brother Zack
ran the famous traveling Wild West show known as
the Miller Brothers' 101 Ranch. A unit of the show
was wintering in California and Balshofer made a
deal to use the 101 Ranch cowboys, Indians, and
stock in a series of westerns filmed under the Bison
brand, a New York Motion Picture Company
subsidiary. Later the name was changed to the
101-Bison brand.

This gave Kessel and Bauman a tremendous
advantage in selling the films. No other company

had such authentic casts, costumes, and props.
Even after paying the Miller Brothers a royalty, the
New York Motion Picture Company declared
twelve-hundred dollars weekly dividends to Kessel,
Bauman, and Balshofer.

This encouraged Kessel and Bauman to expand.
They wired Balshofer in California to return and
help set up a new company to be known as
Keystone. Balshofer was disconcerted to find that
the producer-director of Keystone would be an
ex-boilermaker named Mike Sinnott, who had
decided to call himself Mack Sennett.

In talking with Sennett, Balshofer found out
that Mack had directed a few films for D. W.

12

Griffith at Biograph and had learned about making films by talking to Griffith while walking home each evening with the Biograph producer. He intended, after Keystone was formed, to make pictures about funny cops. Griffith, he said, would never let him do that.

Balshofer was hardly impressed with Sennett's background and ambitions to make funny cop pictures. But, he admitted later, he decided not to object, for he felt that anyone with the gall and gab to convince Addie Kessel and Charlie Bauman to back him was enough of a con man to make a success at just about anything. When the Sennett Keystone Kops became a comedy sensation Balshofer was man enough to admit that he had been wrong about Mack Sennett.

After the details of organizing Keystone were completed, Balshofer remained in New York for a couple of days to discuss business problems with his partners. In the course of the discussions, he told them that they were in for a lot of trouble.

"I was talking today with some connections I have, and Edison is out to break us all," he said.

"Edison has been out to get us ever since we started," Bauman replied. "We're raking in more dough than ever. So what's new?"

Balshofer explained carefully while his partners listened intently. After several years of fighting everybody, Edison had agreed to join the newly formed Motion Picture Patents Company. Members would be licensed to use the Edison patents.

"George Kleine, Sigmund Lubin, William Selig, Essanay, Kalem, Vitagraph, and Pathe are joining. They have Jeremiah J. Kennedy, a Wall Street banker, to head their group."

Kennedy, his enemies said, should have been a buccaneer. He had all the qualifications of a pirate, including an overwhelming desire to make his business enemies walk the plank. Kennedy was working on a plan to stamp out all independent production and force every exhibitor in the country to use only trust films. Each exhibitor would also be required to pay a license fee to the trust for the right to show pictures at all.

"Kennedy is a different man from Edison," Balshofer told his partners. "He intends to smash everybody who doesn't throw in with the trust. They're a closed group now. We can't get in if we wanted to."

"In the past," Balshofer told his partners, "there wasn't enough money involved for the Edison forces to take much legal action. Court cases cost more than they could hope to gain. So they sicked goons on us to smash our cameras and harass our people out of business. We got away from them by moving operations to remote areas. Now things are changing fast.

"The number of theaters are growing. Making pictures has become a very profitable business, as we three well know. It is now worth Kennedy's trouble to take us to court. And that is what he intends to do. He's going to smother us with a mountain of expensive court actions. He expects to bankrupt us. And he can do it."

"So?" Addie Kessel asked softly.

"Edison combined with his new partners in the Motion Picture Patents Company to get strength to dominate the field and gain a complete monopoly," Balshofer replied. "We independents must do the same thing. If we organize into one company, all of us together would finance a single law suit, while as individuals we'd have to fight and pay alone. It would cut our legal expenses eighty percent."

"Go on," Addie said.

"That would reduce our legal expenses to the point where we could afford to fight in court. Now we might lose. Edison *does* own the patents, but there's a strong move in congress to break up trusts. So we got a fighting chance. And if we don't win, we can keep appealing and stalling through the courts. That'll drag things out for years, guaranteeing that we'll stay in business for another five to ten years."

"How will we come out in a merger?" Bauman asked.

"As I see it, each of us who joins the independent group would throw all his assets into the pot. Then we each draw stock in the new company according to the amount of assets we put in. We have the largest assets. We would draw the most stock."

"So we'd be in a position to run things, huh?" Kessel said.

"Sounds good," Bauman added. "But the big question in my mind is, just who would our partners be?"

"Carl Laemmle's IMP is the biggest independent producer after us. Then there's Pat Powers and his Powers Company, Mark Dintenfass and the Champion Company, David Horsley's Nestor, Bill Swanson's Rex, and Eclair. I forget who runs it."

"Charlie Jourjon, I think," Bauman said. "And I believe that Edwin S. Porter has a finger in Rex, along with Joe Engel."

Addie Kessel shook his head. "Nothing doing!" he snapped. "You bring that bunch of Irish and Jews together and they would be cutting each other's throats in a week. They ain't got class like me and you and Charlie."

On that note the meeting broke up and Balshofer went back to Los Angeles to prepare their Edendale property to receive the Mack Sennett Keystone group when it arrived in March. He was immediately plunged into trouble before the Keystone company got its first California picture in the can. (Keystone had previously made one film at Coney Island before coming West.) Some male members of the Keystone company got into trouble over an underage actress. Those accused by the district attorney of statutory rape were in such a position that their arrest would have brought Keystone to a complete halt. Sennett hurriedly assembled Mabel Normand, his leading lady and *not* the girl involved in the morals charge, his leading comedian Ford Sterling, co-director Henri "Pathe" Lehrman, and other members of the cast. They made a mad dash for Mexico where they

David Horsley's Nestor Studio, opened in a former tavern at Gower and Sunset, was the first motion picture studio in Hollywood. Nestor was one of the companies that joined to form the Universal Film Manufacturing Company. Horsley opened October 27, 1911.

set up a temporary studio in Tijuana to escape the Los Angeles police.

Balshofer became so involved in trying to square the charge with the district attorney's office and managing the 101-Bison studio, where Thomas H. Ince was directing westerns, that he completely forgot his suggestion for an independent group merger.

But then in May 1912 he received a wire from New York to return and sign the merger papers. Charlie Bauman had casually mentioned Balshofer's idea to Carl Laemmle. Laemmle was so enthused that he took over and handled negotiations with the other independent producers. He brought the plan back to Bauman and Kessel just as Jeremiah J. Kennedy began filing lawsuits. The two ex-bookies suddenly decided that the merger provided them the best means of fighting the trust. They wired Balshofer to come to New York.

The signing took place in New York on June 2, 1912. The new company, in accordance with Laemmle's suggestion, was named the Universal Film Manufacturing Company. It was composed of the assets of the New York Motion Picture Company, the Independent Motion Picture Company (IMP), Powers Company, Nestor, Champion, Eclair, Yankee, and Rex.

The new partners elected a temporary slate of officers, pending a formal election later in the year. They agreed on Charlie Bauman as the temporary president and Carl Laemmle as the temporary treasurer. Laemmle was picked for treasurer because he was the only one the group trusted with money.

Some of the partners had earlier been associated with the Motion Picture Distributing and Sales Company. This organization, which included Laemmle, Powers, Bauman, and Swanson, among others, had been organized to distribute members' films. Members did nothing but quarrel and accuse the others of robbing them. They did, however, gain a respect for Carl Laemmle's honesty, although they distrusted his ambitions.

Balshofer returned to Los Angeles. Thomas H. Ince was practically running 101-Bison single-handedly and doing such a good job that Balshofer spent most of his time trying "to clean up the Keystone mess," as he called it. Mack Sennett was sulking at Balshofer's interference and denouncing Bauman and Kessel for not releasing the films sent back by the fugitive group in Tijuana. Balshofer refused to make any release as long as there was a chance that Ford Sterling and Pathe Lehrman, the director, might be indicted by the Los Angeles District Attorney. In the meantime, back in New York, Universal added some more brands: Republic, Ambrosio, Itala, and Gem.

Bauman and Kessel congratulated themselves on their first step in controlling the new company. They began plans to cut out Laemmle, Powers, Dintenfass, Horsley, and Swanson. Unfortunately for them, Carl Laemmle had similar ideas and was a smarter businessman. Bauman and Kessel felt secure because they controlled the largest block of stock in Universal. Laemmle countered this by making a deal with Bill Swanson and Pat Powers, two men who were just as tough as Bauman and Kessel. This was the last thing Charlie and Ad expected. Laemmle, Swanson, and Powers had never gotten along before. Swanson and Powers knew they were going to have to side with one of the factions and they preferred Uncle Carl to Ad and Charlie.

Bill Swanson came up out of the rough world of the carnival. He was no stranger to savage in-fighting. While working as a carny pitchman, he met Edwin S. Porter, who was then touring with an Edison projector to show the first motion pictures in rural areas. This acquaintance led Swanson into the film exchange business. When Edison cut off film supplies to independent exchanges, Swanson teamed with Joe Engel (with a secret boost from Edwin S. Porter) to form Rex Films. Porter, because of his connection with Edison, did not want to publicly acknowledge his association with Rex.

Pat Powers, like Swanson, was another tough promoter. He started his working career as a blacksmith. Later he became a labor organizer at a time when muscle was the prime requirement for such a job. Still later he became a phonograph salesman for Edison. While in this work he became associated with Porter and picked up enough knowledge of Porter's work to quit and form his own Powers Picture Plays Company in competition with his formidable ex-boss, Thomas A. Edison.

With two belligerent Irishmen like these on his side, Laemmle made his move at the end of June 1912. A board meeting was called and Charlie Bauman was voted out as president. Ad Kessel wasn't at the meeting, but he wasn't needed— Charlie yelled loud enough for both of them. He tried to rally the other partners behind him. But David Horsley of Nestor, Mark Dintenfass of Champion, Charlie Jourjon of Eclair, and William Steiner, who represented Yankee, backed Laemmle.

Even in this permissive age the language that tradition claims Mr. Bauman employed in discussing the ancestry, morals, and business activity of his partners could not be published. Somewhere in his tirade he managed to get out the information that Bauman and Kessel were pulling their companies out of Universal.

Laemmle retorted that Bauman and Kessel had signed contracts to pool their assets in Universal. These contracts were binding.

"You and Ad can leave the *management* of Universal if you wish," Uncle Carl said firmly. "But your companies stay *in* the Universal. You've got your stock. You'll continue to share in the profits, but you can't run the company! If you don't want to go along with the clear majority, then we'll buy your stock. But you can't take your companies back."

"The hell we can't!" Bauman stormed, beating on the conference table with his fist. "You SOBs are looking for a fight. You damn well got one!"

As Charlie Bauman stormed out, Swanson and Engel left right behind him. Swanson caught the train to California with orders to get Fred Balshofer to join them or throw him out and take over the 101-Bison and Keystone operations himself. Joe Engel of Rex had similar orders to seize the New York operations of Bauman and Kessel.

What happened next is confused by tradition, legend, ego stories of principals, and just plain invention. *The Moving Picture World*, one of the top trade magazines of the time, said, "There were sensational doings in New York and Los Angeles, in efforts to obtain physical possession of the plants."

Movie Historian Terry Ramsaye, in *A Million and One Nights*, claimed there was a two-day battle for possession of the New York Laboratory. Fred Balshofer, as he did on several occasions, disagreed with Ramsaye. Fred claimed there was a minor skirmish at the laboratory, which the police broke up. Two men were arrested for fighting.

On the West Coast, Swanson, Ramsaye, and Balshofer all told different stories. Ramsaye claimed Thomas H. Ince protected Inceville, the 101-Bison headquarters, with a Civil War cannon.

Balshofer claimed the cannon was only a prop. Swanson said his group, who went to take possession of Inceville, had to draw back when Ince and Balshofer got the 101-Ranch cowboys and Indians to come to their aid. This latter story is suspect because the 101-Ranch group wintered in California and were on the road with the traveling Wild West show in the summer. This affair happened in July.

But if Swanson had no luck taking over Inceville, he scored a temporary victory at Edendale where Keystone was headquartered. Edendale, a movie slum, had been vacated by Ince when he moved to Inceville. It was now empty since the Keystone group was in Tijuana still dodging warrants for three of the company on statutory rape charges resulting from the alleged "gang bang" of the sixteen-year-old actress.

Swanson muscled his way past Fred Mace, who had been left in charge of the Edendale plant. He turned Mace out, removed all the locks, and put new ones on. He then returned to Los Angeles to plot a new attack on Inceville. Mace immediately phoned Balshofer, who rushed out and broke the Swanson locks with a sledge hammer. He reinstalled his own locks and hired armed guards to patrol the property.

Laemmle, frustrated in taking over by force, now turned to the courts. He had a perfect case. Bauman and Kessel had delivered their assets to Universal. All they were entitled to by law was their share of the profits.

But early in their bookmaking career, Bauman and Kessel had learned that hiring the best lawyers was the key to success in the kind of businesses they pursued. Now their lawyers, going over the contracts word by word looking for flaws, discovered that Fred Balshofer had not signed the contract transferring New York Motion Picture Company assets to Universal. Somehow, with so many people signing that day, his signature had been overlooked. Since he was NYMP's secretary-treasurer, the contract was void without his signature. Or so their lawyers claimed.

In any event, they had a good enough case that Laemmle's lawyers advised him to compromise. So in a court-approved settlement in October 1912, it was agreed that all physical property belonging to the New York Motion Picture Company would remain in possession of Bauman, Kessel, and Balshofer. However, the company name,

101-Bison, would become the property of Universal. The lawyers asked if Laemmle also wanted the Keystone trademark. Uncle Carl was horrified, for he had heard of the statutory rape charge in California. Also, he was of the firm opinion that Mack Sennett should never have left the boiler-making profession. He wanted no part of anything connected with Sennett.

"If they try to make us take Keystone, sue them!" he told the lawyers.

With this settlement in October 1912, Carl Laemmle became "Mr. Universal," a position he held for the next twenty-four years when he retired in 1936.

Bauman and Kessel made a distribution deal through Mutual and renamed their lost 101-Bison operations Broncho. Balshofer continued with Bauman and Kessel until they joined Triangle in 1916. Uneasy about the financing and stock sales of Triangle, Balshofer pulled out to join Universal as an independent producer releasing through Laemmle.

Laemmle and his quiet but highly efficient partner, Robert H. Cochrane, settled down to battle their partners, grind out pictures, and make Universal live up to its slogan of "the largest film manufacturing company in the universe."

2 Laemmle and the IMP

Mr. Universal was born on January 27, 1867, in Laupheim, Germany, where his father was an estate agent. He went to school until he was thirteen and then was placed with a retail merchant as an apprentice. He rose to be bookkeeper by the time he was sixteen, and a year later sailed for America to join his brother, Joseph. He claimed that his steerage ticket from Bremerhaven, Germany, to New York cost $22.50.

Laemmle worked in stores in New York and Chicago and finally became bookkeeper for the Continental Clothing Company in Oshkosh, Nebraska. The company was owned by Sam Stern of Chicago. Laemmle later married Stern's pretty niece, Recha, and by 1898 had become manager of the Oshkosh store.

The marriage had nothing to do with the appointment. Laemmle was, in the language of the day, a go-getter. The company thrived under his management. He introduced window displays instead of just jamming stuff in the window, and he was especially interested in proper advertising.

This interest in advertising led him directly into his future in the motion picture industry. He began buying advertising mats and cuts from an agency in Chicago. His contact in the agency was a young man named Robert H. Cochrane. Cochrane, born in 1879, was a former newspaper man who brought a terse journalistic style to ad writing, which pleased Laemmle. Laemmle would write Cochrane and tell him what he wanted and Cochrane would respond with the properly worded ad.

In 1905 Laemmle, seeing forty just ahead, decided that he was not getting ahead fast enough. He went to Chicago to see Sam Stern. Ramsaye leaves the impression that Laemmle's unhappiness was due to interference by Stern relatives in the way Laemmle ran the business. Laemmle himself gave a different story. He said that he was displeased because Stern relatives working in the store got what he thought was too large a commission on their sales. He thought he, as manager, should get more and they less.

Stern saw no reason for increasing his manager's stake. He said so in forceful language. Laemmle replied just as forcefully. When he left the Stern home he was the ex-manager of the Continental Clothing Company's Oshkosh store.

Laemmle had done well in Oshkosh and had been able to save a few dollars. He went to Chicago looking for some kind of work. His first stop was at the advertising agency to see Bob Cochrane. Although Cochrane was twelve years Laemmle's junior, the older man had come to rely strongly on Cochrane's advice. Cochrane advised him to go into business for himself.

"No man ever got rich working for somebody else," Cochrane said.

Lemmle agreed. They discussed possibilities. Cochrane suggested that Laemmle try to buy some poorly managed store in Chicago. With his demonstrated ability, he could expect to put the floundering business back on its feet. This was preferable, Cochrane said, to trying to start a new business.

Laemmle started walking around the neighborhood, looking for possibilities. His attention was caught by a store theater. Moving pictures, which had been invented a few years before by Thomas A. Edison, had overgrown their original peepshow status and were now being projected onto screens. Theaters to show the films were made by converting empty stores.*

Since the production of *The Great Train Robbery* two years before, these moving pictures had turned from simple animated snapshots to storytelling featurettes. Laemmle, his entire life absorbed in business, had never even seen one, but now his business sense was aroused at the number of people he saw waiting around the door for the show to open.

He paid a nickel and went in. In later years he was unable to recall what the picture was. He did remember that there was no advertising posters or pictures in the lobby. A handpainted banner proclaimed the name of the picture. The actors were not identified.

He made some discreet inquiries. He learned that it cost very little to put up a store theater. It required only a rented store and a projector, which could be obtained for about $250. Remodeling consisted only of blocking out the windows, building a lobby and box office, and lining the projection booth with zinc sheets to conform with the fire prevention code. If one wanted to be extravagant, he could put in fans for the summer and heaters for the winter. Films could be bought from Biograph for twelve cents a running foot or could be rented at much less from film exchanges. These were companies who bought films outright and tried to make a profit by renting them to exhibitors.

William T. Rock, later a Vitagraph partner, is credited with opening the first store theater. This

was in New Orleans. Epes Winthrop Sargent, the writer, said the first in New York showed a prizefight film. "The exact location is a mystery," he said. "but Arthur D. Hotaling believes it to have been at 204 Broadway, and remembers that it was a couple of steps down from the sidewalk. New York did not take kindly to the store show and it did not progress there until after 1905."

The show Laemmle saw consisted of five short subjects, none of which was over one-hundred feet in length. There were also two illustrated songs in which a baritone was accompanied by color story slides.

Laemmle decided he could set up his own store show for about twelve-hundred dollars investment. After renting and remodeling the premises, the only expenses would be film rental, a dollar-a-day pay for a projectionist, and the salary of a ticket seller. He would not have to invest in stock to sit on the shelf until it was sold. His product, pictures on a screen, would be turned over each day. This looked better than the dry goods business.

Laemmle talked over the idea with Bob Cochrane. The advertising man was not enthusiastic. "You had best talk to someone who knows this business," he cautioned. "I know Bill Swanson, who is in the film exchange business here in Chicago. I'll give you an introduction to him. He's been in the business since it first started."

Laemmle found Bill Swanson the type of man eager to brag of his accomplishments. The impatient little man from Oshkosh had to listen to Swanson tell about his "black top days."

In 1897 Swanson decided that instead of traveling around the country putting on shows in auditoriums at night like Porter, he would do good by setting up moving picture shows in a tent along with other carnival sideshows.

The tent, of course, had to be dark and there was no such thing as black canvas. He couldn't paint the tent black, for then it couldn't be rolled up and moved. He finally succeeded in getting a tent maker to dye one for him. He then opened the first "black top" theater at a carnival in Booneville, Indiana, in July 1897.

"Owing to the extreme difficulty in trying to convince people of the nature of the show or what a moving picture meant, it was fully 9:30 or 10 o'clock before I was able to persuade a dozen people to buy tickets," Swanson said.

*Much has been written in recent years to prove that credit for inventing movies belongs to Dickson, Edison's assistant. Regardless of who did the work, it was Edison's ideas, basic work, and direction that led to practical motion pictures. Despite debunking, he remains the inventor of motion pictures.

"After that, business proceeded nicely until the next Thursday afternoon about two o'clock. A tremendous rainstorm lasted about an hour. When the sun came out my former 'Black Dome' was the whitest tent on the lot and the gutters flowed with black ink!"

It took Swanson another month to obtain a rain-proof dye job to get him back in business. Later he went into store shows and branched out into exchanges.

"Exchanges," he told Laemmle, "is where the money is. When you buy film, it is no good to you after you show it. You got to get out and swap it with some other exhibitor. That takes time. Now the exchange manager buys a film and rents it to a lot of exhibitors. He makes plenty."

Laemmle soaked up what Swanson told him. He learned, among other things, that the illustrated songs didn't cost the exhibitor a cent. Song publishers furnished them to plug their current hits, hoping patrons would then buy the sheet music (at a dime) to play on the parlor piano. Charles K. Harris, author of the great hit *"After the Ball (Is Over),"* originated the idea.

Laemmle was sold, but delayed several days while he visited Chicago's other theaters to check their patronage. "I was sitting in the Nickeloden on Halsted Street near Van Buren when I definitely made up my mind," Laemmle told a reporter in 1916.

He found an empty store at 909 Milwaukee Avenue and had it remodeled. An old photograph, too poor to reproduce here, shows it to have been thirty feet wide. The box office was in the center of a shallow lobby with an entrance door on the right and an exit on the left. There were no posters, except a hand-painted announcement above the box office. The fringe on the awning said, "Coolest 5 cent Theater in Chicago." The announcement about the temperature must have been put up later, for the White Front Theater opened for business on February 24, 1906 when coolness wasn't needed.

The first program was a nine-hundred-foot Biograph film and an illustrated song slide. The name of the film has been lost.

Laemmle claimed in a 1917 interview that the theater averaged $180. a day. This does not appear likely. The theater seated 214, if every seat was filled. A nine-hundred-foot film, plus an illustrated song number added to the time needed to empty and refill the house made it unlikely that he could have shown more than two showings per hour. He would have had to fill the theater to capacity for eight straight hours a day to have made this gross.

It would have required thirty-six-hundred patrons a day at five cent a ticket to add up to $180 in receipts. What is probable is that Laemmle confused the receipts from the White Front nickel theater with his Family Theater, started later, which charged a dime.

His total outlay was four-hundred dollars for remodeling, twenty-five dollars for a plaster-covered muslin screen, $250 for seats, and $250 for the projector. Other expenses included a business license, advance rent, salaries for a projectionist and ticket seller, and miscellaneous small expenses. His total investment was about twelve-hundred dollars. This included his first day's film rental of three dollars.

He recouped his investment the first month. After that his expenses never totaled more than $150 a week and his take was never less than six-hundred dollars. This success whetted his ambition. In April 1906, two months after he opened the White Front, Laemmle hired Walther Johnson to manage the White Front while he opened the Family Theater at 1233 Halstead Street.

He had noted that rival shows were dark, hot, and dirty. Laemmle put in huge fans, kept his place clean, and hired a muscle man to throw out rowdy elements at his Family Theater. A strong advertising campaign by Cochrane brought in the family trade at a ten cent admission price.

Laemmle's big problem was getting film. Exchanges were unreliable. Delivery service was poor and prints were often brittle and scratched. Sometimes they didn't have what he ordered and made unauthorized substitutions.

He remembered Swanson's advice that exchanges, rather than theaters, was the way to make money in the movie business, but his decision to enter the exchange business was to ensure his own film supply. He got Cochrane to write him some direct mail ads in which he pointed out the deficiencies of the ordinary exchange. He promised clean prints and reliable delivery.

Like his two theaters, good business practices ensured initial success. Business boomed so much that Laemmle, dropping in to get Cochrane to write some new ads, complained to his friend that he wished he had the money to expand further. All his ready cash had gone into film stocks for the exchange.

"Would twenty-five hundred dollars help?" Cochrane asked.

Laemmle envisioned how many new reels of film that would buy at twelve cents a foot and said it sure would. They dickered for a few minutes and Laemmle left with Cochrane's check for twenty-five hundred dollars. The advertising man received ten percent of the Laemmle business, starting an association that lasted through both their motion picture careers.

Laemmle bought from every manufacturer, ensuring a variety of films available. Robert H. Cochrane, reminiscing in the March 10, 1917, issue of *Motion Picture World,* said he and Laemmle would not send out a single reel to an exhibitor "unless furnished with a bank guaranty covering the cost of the film, for that was the custom in those days.

"In the old days there was an overwhelming mass of petty jealousies, personal hatred and fostered bitterness. It was impossible to get any very considerable group of exchange men or producers or exhibitors to work together for the common good, because each of us thought the other had an ulterior motive. And each of us was generally right!"

Cochrane's statement amply described the men who later formed Universal.

Laemmle and Cochrane were bears for work. Word of their square dealing got around and their exchange business boomed until by 1909 the Laemmle Film Service was the largest exchange in the United States and the biggest buyer of films the producers had.

The world looked rosy to Carl Laemmle on January 1, 1909, but a shock awaited him. Thomas A. Edison, after fighting for years to prove his ownership of basic motion picture patents, received a court decision supporting his patent claims. The result was the formation of the Motion Picture Patents Company. The group included Edison and the so-called licensed companies who had his permission to use Edison patents.

The booming motion picture industry thought this "trust," as it came to be known, was intended to stamp out independent producers, such as Bauman, Kessel, Balshofer, and others. Vitagraph, Lubin, Essanay, among others, were members of the trust. Laemmle and Cochrane were not overly

concerned. The Laemmle Film Service was the largest single buyer of trust film. You don't pick on your best customer, or so Laemmle thought. But Laemmle did not know Jeremiah J. Kennedy.

The blockbuster came when the Film Service Association met to discuss mutual problems in January 1909. The Film Service Association was a group of exchange owners so honest that Bill Swanson, the association president, refused to accept dues checks from any of them. This was because three-fourths of the checks bounced. We have this on the authority of Robert H. Cochrane. In any dealing with this group, Cochrane himself demanded cash and carefully inspected the bills before he accepted them.

The shock the Film Service Association members got was in the form of a neatly printed folder that listed the Motion Picture Patents Company's new policy toward exchanges and exhibitors. Edison was out to control the entire motion picture industry, including production, distribution, and exhibition.

Frank L. Dyer of Edison then explained more details of the trust plan. All licensed producers would pay a fee to Edison for the privilege of using his patents. Exchanges would also be required to pay a license fee. Each exhibitor would also be required to pay a two dollar-a-week fee to use Edison projectors in his theater. Producers were forbidden to sell their films to unlicensed exchanges. Licensed exchanges were forbidden to rent film to unlicensed exhibitors. Any who violated these rules would be sued in court and would lose their licenses.

The majority felt that they had no alternative but to pay. The courts had recently ruled in favor of Edison on his patent claims. Bill Swanson, in colorful carnival language, expressed his opinion of Edison's ancestry and informed all who would listen of his opinion where Edison, Jeremiah J. Kennedy, and all members of the trust could go. He announced to the trade the next day that he was going independent. He would buy film from unlicensed producers and rent it to unlicensed exhibitors.

Swanson made his announcement on March 20, 1909, after assuring himself that there would be enough independent production to keep his exchange going. At the same time he began plans to start his own company, Rex. Other exchangemen sided with Swanson.

Laemmle, despite his independence, did not immediately do so. He had the largest exchange system in the United States and was the trust's biggest customer. He honestly did not feel that they would treat him like the rest. Jeremiah J. Kennedy lumped all nonlicense paying exchangemen in the same category—an unprintable one. Laemmle replied with a formal notice dated April 12, 1909, that he would not pay a trust license, but would operate independently.

Representatives of the trust came to talk to him. Laemmle was adamant. They wanted a fight. He was ready for them. It was not so much the actual license fee that irked him. He discussed the matter with Bob Cochrane who pointed out that the trust's action was aimed at complete control. Already licensed producers were told how long their films would be, how much they would charge, and how many prints they could make of each production. This schedule was set up to keep down competition among the nine trust producers.

"Producers in the trust will never make any real money." Cochrane argued. "Kennedy and the Edison forces will keep squeezing the profits. This license fee is just the beginning. We might as well get out than join them."

This was the kind of argument Laemmle understood. He did not want to work in a closed monopoly. Competition was in his blood. He did not fear it. He had competed with other dry goods merchants in Oshkosh and beat them at their own game.

"I am sure exhibitors will buy from us, trust or no trust," Cochrane said. "But the big question—and we'll rise or fall on it—is whether Edison can put the independent producers out of business."

"Can he do it?" Laemmle inquired.

"Not in the courts," Cochrane said, "It takes forever to try to civil case and then a smart lawyer can drag it through appeals for years. If I were in J. J. Kennedy's place, I'd hire some bully boys and wreck the independent's cameras. That would put them out of business."

Laemmle thought this over. He knew Cochrane was right. He also knew that Kennedy was capable of such direct action. Suddenly he made his decision.

"If Edison and Kennedy stop our film supplies, we'll make our own pictures!" he said positively.

President Theodore Roosevelt had led a strong government attack on trusts and monopolies. While President Taft, who succeeded Roosevelt, had not done as much, public temper was still against trusts, which in the case of oil had jacked up prices enormously. The Democratic party, which seemed in a fair way to win the 1912 election, was pledged to do more "trust busting." In this climate, Laemmle felt that he could hold his own against the Edison forces. But only if he had public support.

He went after it with an enormous advertising campaign. every word written by Cochrane. He sneered, poked fun, and exposed every mistake of the trust. Cochrane's ads have become a legend.

The Trust formed the General Film Company to control its licensed producers, and act as the releasing agency for them all. Cochrane burlesqued the name by using a fat army officer he called "General Flimco."

One of the early ads written by Cochrane and signed by Laemmle showed a fat plutocrat collecting two dollars from a line of poor exhibitors. A pile of money, labeled "one million dollars a year," overflows his coffers. The written material ran:

"COME OUT OF IT, MR. EXHIBITOR! Are you going to pay $2 a week every week you are in business for the right to run your own theater and use your own goods?"

The trust struck back by threatening theater owners who used films from the Laemmle exchange. Uncle Carl and Bob Cochrane replied by publishing threatening letters written by the trust to exhibitors. Then in an editorial in an exchange paper and through handbills sent to theater owners, Laemmle said:

"The trust is threatening exhibitors with 'fines and calamities' for running my films. Take it from me, if any fines or calamities are imposed upon any customer of mine, I'll back the exhibitor with all the resources at my command. I'll fight his fight for him or bust myself! If anyone comes into your place and tries to scare you with any sort of bluff, hand him one swift, speedy kick in the seating capacity and I'll pay the damages."

These were brave words, but Laemmle faced a serious problem. This was film to rent. He couldn't buy trust film anymore. The independents who sprang up were being rapidly put out of business by Edison's lawyers. Fred Balshofer had just been closed and so had Bill Swanson who had rushed into independent production. The "outlaw" films that Laemmle could buy were of poor quality and far from being "the best films available," which Laemmle had promised his trade. He realized that this would soon put him out of business, even if the one-hundred lawsuits filed against the Laemmle Film Service didn't close him up first.

The only solution to the film problem was to go into production himself. He broke with the trust on April 12, 1909, and announced his decision to produce pictures in June of the same year. He rented a studio at 111 East 14th Street, New York (not to be confused with Biograph's famous address, 11 East 14th Street). He hired William Ranous, who had worked with Biograph and William Ranous, who had worked with Biograph and Lubin, to be his director. But before Ranous could begin, Kennedy swore out an injunction against Laemmle to halt filming.

Acting on the suggestion of James Bryson, an exchange employee, Laemmle told Ranous to go to some remote spot where Kennedy's spies couldn't find him. Ranous took a second-hand camera Laemmle had bought at a bankruptcy auction, hired some actors, and set out for Minneapolis, Minnesota, to film *Hiawatha* against the natural background of Minnehaha Falls.

Gladys Hulette, who achieved her greatest fame with Richard Barthelmess in *Tol'able David,* played the Indian maiden Minehaha. William Ranous took the role of Hiawatha. Later both Laemmle and King Baggott claimed that Baggott was the company's first actor, but both seem to have forgotten Ranous's Indian role. Baggott, however, was certainly the first star of Laemmle's new company.

King Baggott was born in St. Louis, Missouri, in 1880, and had played in stock for several years. He managed to make Broadway in a supporting role in one of Marguerite Clark's plays. He went on tour with the Clark company, but when it folded he was glad to accept William Ranous's offer to join the new Laemmle company.

While Ranous was in Minnesota filming *Hiawatha,* Laemmle ran a contest for a name for the new company. He had originally called it Yankee Films, but decided to change it when Bob Cochrane pointed out that the name might hamper sales in the Deep South where they still pronounced Yankee as "Damyankee."

Two people submitted "The Independent Moving Picture Company" suggestion, but Laemmle chose the one sent by John Mapes of New York because Mapes had accompanied the suggestion with a clever cartoon showing a little devil spreading out his cloak, which was over-printed with the initials IMP.

And so IMP films was born, and the first release set for October 25. Cochrane wrote the ad: "At

King Baggott was the first leading man hired by Laemmle's IMP. An extremely versatile actor, he starred in an unusually wide variety of roles during his twelve years with Laemmle.

Last! At Last! With a soul full of hope and a heart full of pride and enthusiasm, I now announce the FIRST RELEASE OF "IMP FILMS on Monday, October 25th!

"I present 'HIAWATHA'. Length 988 feet. Taken at the Falls of Minnehaha in the Land of the Dacotahs. And you can bet it is classy or I wouldn't make it my first release. It is taken from Longfellow's masterpiece of poesy. It is a gem of photography and acting. Get *'Hiawatha'* and see if

King Baggott, as this 1916 ad shows was an extremely versatile actor. He also doubled as a director.

you don't agree that it starts a brand new era in American moving pictures."

He went on to promise that IMP would produce the best pictures that "man's skill can execute. And no cheating on measurements."

3 The IMP Runs Wild

It took Laemmle almost four months to get *Hiawatha* from concept to screen, but he lost no time after that. IMP produced a picture a week for the remainder of 1909. The following year, operating three production crews, IMP released one-hundred films, while fighting the trust's goons with goons of their own and dodging process servers with new lawsuits.

In late 1910 IMP got its most famous director. He was a chubby little man who was not doing so well as an actor. His name was Thomas H. Ince.

Ince's family were actors and he grew up in child parts, but he matured into a man with a short, dumpy figure that looked anything but heroic. He did manage some supporting work, including a part in the 1903 production of *Hearts Courageous,* a revolutionary war play with Orrin Johnson. William S. Hart had the role of Patrick Henry in the play and this was the beginning of a friendship that later resulted in Hart becoming a movie actor.

In October 1910 Ince met Joe Smiley, who was working for IMP. Smiley got Tom Cochrane, Bob's brother, to take Ince on in a heavy role. He made one picture and then went to Biograph for one picture. His wife, Alice Kershaw, had been working there for "Old Man" McCutcheon. He went back to IMP, but kept pestering Tom Cochrane, who was managing IMP's New York production, while brother Bob and Laemmle held down the fort in Chicago, to let him direct. Ince knew very well that he would never do much as an actor.

The year 1910 was also the time that Laemmle made his famous raid on Biograph and stole away the rival company's brightest star. She was Florence Lawrence, the wife of Harry Salter, who played heavies and did some directing for Biograph.

Biograph did not identify its casts. H. N. Marvin, the manager, had no intention of letting stars develop as they had on the stage. Stars cost money and that cut into producers' profits. The public insisted on making its own stars, and liked Miss Lawrence better than any of the other Biograph actresses, including the girl with the curls they knew only as Little Mary, Mary Pickford. Thus Florence Lawrence became the Biograph Girl.

Laemmle made a personal trip to New York from Chicago to talk to Miss Lawrence. He promised her billing and a major raise in pay. She gave H. N. Marvin and his director, D. W. Griffith, her notice.

Mr. Bob Cochrane, who was still writing IMP's publicity, then put out a story that Miss Lawrence had been killed in an accident in St. Louis. She was identified in the publicity as the former Biograph Girl.

This done, the enterprising Mr. Cochrane wrote a follow-up story blasting his previous story as a dirty trick of the trust, since the former Biograph Girl was now an IMP. Furthermore, to prove to the good people of St. Louis that this was true, Miss Lawrence, accompanied by that sterling IMP actor,

Mr. King Baggott, would make a personal appearance in St. Louis.

So far as anyone can determine this was the first big publicity gimmick dreamed up by a studio press agent and the first formal personal appearance by an acknowledged movie star. Baggott and Miss Lawrence were mobbed by their admiring fans. After appearances in two St. Louis theaters, who booked IMP features, they returned to New York to star in a series of pictures together.

Miss Lawrence soon tired of the hectic life of grinding out films for IMP. She declined to renew her contract and retired. Her pictures had made money. In addition the raid on Biograph resulted in marvelous publicity for IMP, besides being a dig at the trust.

Laemmle now set out to repeat himself by raiding Biograph for Little Mary (Pickford). Negotiations were carried on with Mrs. Charlotte Pickford (Smith), Mary's mother. Those who disliked Mrs. Pickford—and they were considerable in number—said she was born with a cash register in the place of a heart and that Little Mary was a true daughter of her mother.

In any event, Mary Pickford signed with IMP for $175 a week and the promise of billing that she had never gotten at Biograph. Miss Pickford, on her own without Mrs. Pickford's knowledge, insisted that IMP employ Owen Moore as well. Owen, an extremely handsome man, was a member of a trio of Irish brothers that included Tom and Matt. He was, unknown to both Laemmle and Mrs. Pickford, secretly married to Mary.

Harry Salter, who had been directing some IMP films, left when his wife, Florence Lawrence, quit. Thomas H. Ince then became a director and was given Mary Pickford and Owen Moore. The first film Miss Pickford made for IMP was *Their First Misunderstanding*. The title summed up her relations with the Laemmle Company.

Jeremiah J. Kennedy was swinging hard at the independents. Where court actions failed or were drawn out, he sent in goon squads to break cameras, throw rocks at actors, and otherwise disrupt production. At the same time he began using the huge fund of money gathered through the license system to buy up exchanges. Those who refused to sell were cut off on film. Kennedy was out to control the entire industry.

The one bright spot for the independent producers was that George Eastman of Eastman Kodak, the only United States manufacturer of raw motion picture film stock, had been persuaded to break with the trust. Earlier Eastman had agreed to sell film only to producers allied with the trust. Then later his lawyers pointed out that it appeared that the government, egged on by Laemmle and William Fox, another independent, was considering an antitrust charge against the Edison forces. Eastman, by his refusal to sell film to the independents, was also clearly in violation of antitrust laws.

Eastman removed his embargo and began selling raw film to the independents. This enormously increased independent production. Previously they had bought from Jules Brulatour, New York agent for the French firm of Lumieres Brothers. Unfortunately Brulatour was unable to supply all the film the independents needed.

Kennedy's harassment became so bad that the independents fled from New York and Fort Lee, New Jersey, where they were entrenched. Several went out of business. Others went to Florida and California. Hearing that Edison spies were following Balshofer's group to California, Laemmle decided to send his IMP crew completely out of the United States. Doc Willat, a Laemmle employee, was sent to Cuba to find a place for the IMP production there. Shortly after, in the fall of 1910, Ince, Mary Pickford, George Loane Tucker, Owen Moore, Lottie Pickford, Jack Pickford, Charlotte Pickford, King Baggott, J. Farrel Mac Donald, Haywood Mack, Tony Gaudio the cameraman, among others, sailed for Cuba.

Just before they sailed Charlotte Pickford learned that her darling daughter had secretly married "that drunkard" Owen Moore. Mary Pickford in her autobiography said that her mother cried for three days. To make matters worse Thomas H. Ince developed an intense dislike of Owen Moore, a feeling that was shared by a number of other men in the troupe.

None of their tempers was improved by the conditions they had to work under. An Edison lawyer showed up and tried to get an injunction to close them down. Owen Moore was quarreling both with his wife and members of the cast. The situation climaxed in a fight that got Owen Moore jailed. Mary Pickford claimed the fight was because one of the male cast insulted her. Others have claimed it was because of Owen Moore's drunken rudeness. At one point Bob Cochrane had to make

The production unit of IMP in the winter of 1910-11 consisted of (from left, front row) Isabel Rae, Jack Pickford, Lottie Pickford; (second row) Thomas H. Ince, director; Owen Moore, Mary Pickford, King Baggott, Joe Smiley; (Third row) William Shay, Mrs. David Miles, Joe MacDonald, Haywood Mack, Mrs. Joe MacDonald, John Harvey; (back row) George Loane Tucker, David Miles, Mrs. Pickford, Robert Daley, and Tony Gaudio, cameraman.

a trip to Cuba, partly to do some local politicking to keep Edison forces from getting court injunctions to stop the shooting and partly to bring order out of the personality conflicts.

At this point IMP and the Laemmle exchanges were completely dependent upon the output from Cuba to keep going. In all the company had seventy-five people and was trying to get out three one-reelers a week. Mainly because of Mary Pickford's popularity IMP business boomed. The first film. made before going to Cuba *(Their First Misunderstanding),* was not released until January 9, 1911. The brochure, *Tribute to Mary Pickford,*

published by the American Film Institute and based on records of the Mary Pickford Corporation, lists thirty-four Pickford film for IMP. There is some conflict between this listing and Universal records.

The Pickford list and release dates were given as:

Their First Misunderstanding, Jan. 9, 1911
The Dream, Jan. 23, 1911
Maid or Man, Jan. 30, 1911
At the Duke's Command, Feb. 6, 1911
The Mirror, Feb. 9, 1911
While the Cat's Away, Feb. 9, 1911
Her Darkest Hour, Feb. 13, 1911

Artful Kate, Feb. 23, 1911
A Manly Man, Feb. 27, 1911
The Message in the Bottle, March 9, 1911
The Fisher-Maid, March, 16, 1911
In Old Madrid, March 20, 1911
Sweet Memories, March 27, 1911
The Stampede, April 17, 1911
Second Sight, May 1, 1911
The Fair Dentist, May 8, 1911
For Her Brother's Sake, May 11, 1911
The Master and the Man, May 15, 1911
The Lighthouse Keeper, May 18, 1911
Back to the Soil, June 8, 1911
In the Sultan's Garden, July 3, 1911
For the Queen's Honor, July 6, 1911
A Gasoline Engagement, July 10, 1911
At a Quarter of Two, July 13, 1911
Science, July 24, 1911
The Skating Bug, July 31, 1911
The Call of the Song, August, 13, 1911
The Toss of a Coin, August 31, 1911
'Tween Two Loves, Sept. 28, 1911
The Rose's Story, Oct. 2, 1911
The Sentinel Asleep, Oct. 9, 1911
The Better Way, Oct. 12, 1911
His Dress Shirt, October 30, 1911
From the Bottom of the Sea, Nov. 20, 1911

Mary Pickford and Owen Moore in one of Thomas H. Ince's IMP films, *The Wife*.

In addition to these, Universal records the following (no original release dates available): *His Gratitude, In Sunny Spain, The Outcome, The Stronger Love,* and *How Mary Fixed It.* Some of these may be reissues with the names changed. In addition *Photoplay* Magazine listed IMP-Pickford-Ince films called *The Wife, The Prince's Portrait,* and *Memories of Yesterday.* In the same story, Julian Johnson, *Photoplay's* editor, said Mary Pickford only made twelve pictures in Cuba. The rest were filmed in New York.

Mary Pickford had been unhappy at IMP. She disliked Thomas H. Ince, for Ince was dictatorial and would brook none of her interference in the filming. In addition, she resented Ince's contemptuous attitude toward her spoiled brother, Jack Pickford. She was also extremely unhappy in her marriage to a man who stayed drunk half the time.

After their return from Cuba, Mary Pickford left IMP in the fall of 1911, joining Reliance. Owen Moore and George Loane Tucker went with her. Laemmle was not too happy at having his star raided as he had raided Biograph.

Shortly after Miss Pickford departed, Thomas H. Ince made a production deal with Kessel, Bauman, and Balshofer's New York Motion Picture Company and departed for California to make pictures under the 101-Bison brand. He worked first at Edendale and then moved to what became known as Inceville near Santa Monica. Balshofer was head of production, but Ince was not a man who took kindly to supervision. After he established himself, Balshofer gave him almost autonomous control of his productions.

The situation with the trust had grown worse, resulting in the consolidation of Powers, Dintenfass, David Horsley, Bill Swanson, and Laemmle into the Universal Film Manufacturing Company in June 1912. By July the new company was gripped in an internal war for control. After Bauman, Kessel, and Balshofer pulled out at the end of June 1912, Horsley, Dintenfass, and finally

Swanson sold their interests to Laemmle. Pat Powers hung on the longest selling out to Laemmle and Cochrane in 1920.

The trouble with the trust now reached its climax. Under President Howard Taft, little had been done, but in the summer of 1912, the Democratic candidate, Woodrow Wilson, came out strongly against trusts of all kinds. Both independent William Fox and Carl Laemmle strongly supported Wilson. The result was that the Republican administration, seeing Wilson's support growing, suddenly began to take action against the trusts whose monopolies were raising prices.

The government did not challenge Edison's patents—these were clear—but charged that the Motion Picture Trust and its exchange system, the General Film Company, used these patents to create a monopoly and that the patent law should not be used to set aside the more important Sherman Antitrust Law.

Edison lawyers fought for delays and the hearings did not occur until April 1914 and the decree breaking the trust was not handed down until 1915. However, the trust was so busy fighting its case with seventeen lawyers that Universal was free from the harassment that had hampered production in the past.

Universal expanded tremendously. Laemmle moved his headquarters from Chicago to New York, taking a floor above his New York film exchange in the Mecca Building at 1600 Broadway.

The Mecca Building exchange, in addition to the offices of the managers, consisted of three rooms. The general office was guarded by a secretary who took the customer's name and directed him to the proper person. Behind her the wall was covered with posters of Universal stars and one-sheets displayed on easels plugging the latest films. A cashier's booth occupied the back of the room where customers settled their bills.

The order room was split in half. One section was the storage bins for films. It had two access windows. One was marked "Films IN," and the other was marked "Films OUT." A long table in the waiting portion permitted customers to inspect the cans of film before leaving.

In another room girls sat at tables and rewound each reel. Films were not rewound when returned to the exchange in order to facilitate inspection. They checked for dirty film, unrepaired breaks, excessive scratches and other evidence of improper care.

In a film exchange this was very important work. Laemmle guaranteed his customers that he would give them good prints, and careless projection by any one renter could ruin a print and make it useless for further projection.

The film care situation was so serious that Laemmle once sent out a flyer to his customers:

WHO is doing the DAMAGE?
We want every operator to read this warning.
Don't get sore, boys, there's nothing personal about this. But read it and if it fits your case, take a friendly tip. Here goes. Some moving picture operators take a brand, new, beautiful and expensive print costing thousands of dollars to produce, and run it through a greasy, dirty, filthy projection machine, till the film is covered with oil and grease and filth and dirty finger marks—practically spoiling it through their habits of laziness, dirtiness or incompetence.
Listen, boys, this isn't right, and you know it. If you are guilty of this, just remember that it's your own reputation that you are blackening. Don't blame your machine. If there is anything the matter with it; if it's in such a rotten condition that you can't use a film without spoiling it—have the boss report it to his exchange. They will help you. They'll loan you a machine while yours is being fixed, if necessary.

At this time Universal pictures were not sold individually, but were marketed as "The Universal Program." For $105 a week an exhibitor got enough Universal films to change programs every day. The program was generally four reels. This included one two-reel drama, one one-reel comedy, and one general-interest one-reeler. The general-interest one-reeler might be anything from an educational feature to a drama or a cartoon. The cartoons were usually split-reels, that is they took up half a reel only to keep down artists' costs, and the other half was frequently a travelogue, such as those made in 1914-15 by Homer Croy on a round-the-world trip.

A typical Universal Program is this one for the week of December 14.

Monday, Dec. 14, 1914
IMP—*The Mill Stream* (two-reel drama) with King Baggott
Victor—*The Wayward Son* (drama)
Sterling—*Lizzie's Fortune* (one-reel comedy) with Max Asher
Tuesday, Dec. 15, 1914
Gold Seal—*The Ghost of Smiling Jim* (two-reel western) Grace Cunard and Francis Ford
Crystal—*Such a Mistake* and *The Glass Pistol* (split-reel)
Nestor—*The Boy Mayor* (one reel) Juvenile drama
Wednesday, Dec. 16, 1914
Joker—*How Father Won Out* (one-reel comedy)

Eclair—*A Game of Wits* (two-reel detective drama) with Carol Hathaway
Animated Weekly—A newsreel (directed by Jack Cohn)
Thursday, Dec. 17, 1914
IMP—*Within the Gates of Paradise* (one-reel Christmas drama)
Rex—*Ambition* (two-reel drama) Ben Wilson and Frances Nelson
Sterling—*The Fatal Hanson* (one-reel comedy)
Friday, Dec. 18, 1914
Nestor—*His Doggone Luck* and *Here and There in Japan* (split-reel)
Powers—No release this week
Victor—*Heart of the Hills*—(three-reel drama) Mary Fuller, Charles Ogle
Saturday, Dec. 19, 1914
Joker—*His Doctor's Orders* (one-reel comedy)
Frontier—Title not decided
101-Bison—*The Christmas Spirit* (two-reel drama) Murdock MacQuarrie
Sunday, Dec. 20, 1914
Rex—*A Page from Life* (two-reel drama) Herbert Rawlinson, Anna Little
L-KO—*The Baron's Bear Escape* (one-reel comedy)
Eclair—*The Jewel of Allah* (one-reel drama) Edna Payne

At this time Universal was supporting fourteen production companies. Twelve of these had joined Universal when the company was formed in June 1912. Two new ones had been added in 1913. One of these was Sterling. Fred Balshofer, who had pulled out of Universal with his partners Kessel and Bauman, became disturbed when Ad and Charlie began talking to Harry Aitkin about forming a new combine that would be financed by sale of stock. He refused to join and set up independent production by stealing Ford Sterling and Pathe Lehrman from Keystone. He then made a deal to release through Universal.

Ford Sterling was an extremely temperamental ex-burlesque comedian who resented any instructions from Lehrman, the director. Lehrman, despite his beginnings in the movie industry, had a first-rate comedy mind. Mack Sennett, although he would never admit it, owed a lot of the initial success of Keystone to Lehrman. It was Lehrman who invented the idea of the Sennett Bathing Beauties after seeing some of the crew whistle at Mabel Normand when she appeared in a one-piece bathing suit. The one-piece bathing suit was very daring for the day. It had just been introduced by Annette Kellerman, the Australian swimmer.

Mr. Lehrman was born in Austria of Jewish parents. Somehow he got to the United States and eventually became a streetcar conductor on the line that ran past 11 E. 14th Street where D. W. Griffith had his Biograph studio.

Henri Lehrman was a very sharp man. He listened to the talk among the Biograph actors who used his car. One day he engaged Arthur Johnson, a Griffith actor, in conversation. He learned that

After breaking with Mack Sennett, Ford Sterling—former chief of the Keystone Kops—joined Pathe Lehrman and Fred Balshofer in independent production for Universal release. Insert shows Ford in the Schultz characterization he used in these films.

Biograph had more actors than they needed, but desperately needed directors to expand. Further investigation showed the astute Mr. Lehrman that the Pathe Brothers in France were highly regarded by Griffith.

A few days later Lehrman told the street car superintendent what he could do with his suspicious supervision and presented himself to D.W. Griffith as a former employee of Pathe. Griffith immediately hired him, but it only took one day to show that Mr. Lehrman had never been inside a

Grace Cunard, playing the daughter, is overjoyed when her long-lost father, Francis Ford, regains his wits after being struck by falling timber during a storm in *The Ghost of Smiling Jim,* a 1914 two-reeler.

Synopsis: Jack Thornby is accused of murdering Tom Craven and convicted on circumstantial evidence that the two had quarreled over Mary Wheatley. Jack is sentenced to twenty years in prison. After he goes to jail Mary is boating on the mill stream when she sees a body caught in the rocks. Coming closer she sees a billfold protruding from the man's pocket which she recognizes as Tom's. She calls the sheriff. The dead man is a tramp who killed Tom for his money and then, in trying to escape, he fell and killed himself on the rocks. Jack is released from prison and he and Mary marry.

This is a story in which the hero does absolutely nothing heroic. The solution of the mystery depends upon an accidental discovery and the chance that a body would remain exposed on rocks for months without being discovered is close to impossible. Nevertheless, Universal plugged the film as a powerful indictment of circumstantial evidence.

Another film on this week's program, *The Ghost of Smiling Jim,* released December 15, 1914, was directed by Francis Ford and starred himself and Grace Cunard. Wilbur Higby played the villain. The

studio before. Instead of firing him, Griffith was amused. He kept him, but nicknamed him Pathe, and Pathe Lehrman he remained for the rest of his life. Rather than resenting the tag, Lehrman adopted the name in his advertising when he became his own producers in later years.

The quarreling between Lehrman and Sterling was more than Balshofer could take. After a year he let Sterling and Lehrman go. He continued to produce under the Sterling banner, while Lehrman got financing to start his own L-KO company for Universal release. L-KO got its name from Lehrman Komedy. Eventually Lehrman did very well with Billie Ritchie, a Chaplin imitator.

A review of the plot outlines of some of the major pictures on the above listed Universal Program for the Week of December 14, 1914, shows that story quality was not high. Coincidence played a major role in the plot solutions.

The Mill Stream was directed by King Baggott with Baggott as Jack Thornby, Arline Pretty as Mary Wheatley, and Robert Hill as Tom Craven.

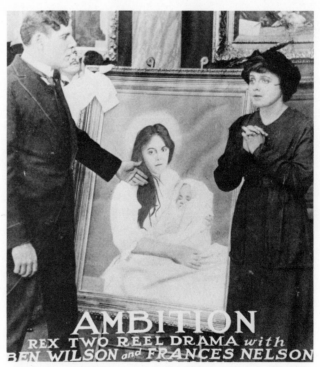

An artist, Ben Wilson, redeems his faithless wife, Frances Nelson, by portraying her as the Madonna in *Ambition,* a 1914 two-reeler that Wilson also directed.

31

story, written by Grace Cunard, is better constructed than *The Mill Stream,* but still relies on coincidence for the denouement.

Synopsis: Higby, played by Wilbur Higby, attempts to jump the mine discovered by Smiling Jim. In the fight Jim is knocked over a cliff. He strikes his head and loses his memory. He then wanders off into the hills where he lives as hermit. As the years pass, people catch only a glimpse of him, giving rise to the story that he is a ghost.

After Smiling Jim disappears, his wife and little daughter live in the town until they are evicted by Higby. One day, now a grown woman, Jim's daughter Grace, is riding in the hills when she sees the "ghost."

A storm comes up and she takes refuge in an old cabin where the ghost also takes refuge. A tree is uprooted by the gale. It crashes through the cabin roof and strikes Jim on the head, restoring his memory. He recognizes his daughter, tells her all that has happened, and together they expose Higby.

Ambition, released December 12, 1914, was directed by Ben Wilson with himself and Frances Nelson in the leading roles. Authorship was not given.

Synopsis; John Willis, a young artist, chooses to marry Marion Davis (Frances Nelson), a selfish actress, instead of Belle LaVeer (Miss Wierman), who really loves him. In time John and Marion have a child, Don (played by Jane Lee), who becomes deathly ill. Selfish Marion leaves the child with its father, from whom she is now separated, while she goes on to the theater. She prefers to neglect her child rather than miss a performance.

The child dies. Almost hysterical with grief, John wanders off where he is comforted by Belle LaVeer. Later, John paints a picture of his erring wife and lost son as the Madonna and Child. The painting receives first prize at an art show. Marion comes to see it and is brokenhearted as she realizes her mistake. Selfless Belle LaVeer, realizing the change in Marion, brings Marion and John together.

These stories came from everywhere. Many were written by the stars themselves or the director and other members of the Universal supervisory team. Universal did not invest a lot of money in already published books, because of the competition of other studios, but they did employ famous writers to turn out originals for the screen. One of these, Louis Joseph Vance, author of the famous Lone Wolf stories, returned the kindness by blasting the treatment his stories got at the hands of directors. The J. Warren Kerrigan Terrence O'Rourke series were written by Vance.

4 Sex and Violence

In 1913 the motion picture industry was split between producers who plugged multireel features and those who wanted to make only shorts.

Adolph Zukor was the staunchest supporter of the feature with his Famous Players in Famous Plays Company. The Lasky Feature Play Company, organized in November 1913, was another.

For years the Motion Picture Patents Company—the trust—had fought feature pictures and even ordered its members not to make them.

Those who favored features insisted that it took the longer length to properly develop character and make a good picture. Those who opposed them did so on economic grounds. If one made a feature and it failed to pull an audience, the program was a total failure. But in a program made up of three different films, such as Universal offered, the audience still had the chance to see something it liked.

Laemmle, for the first and only time in his career, solidly agreed with the trust on features. In both his *Universal Weekly,* a trade publication, and in fliers to exchanges and exhibitors, he denounced the trend toward feature plays.

One of his blasts went like this:

When the first feature man got ready to separate the exhibitor from his money, he made the operation painless for a time by chloroforming him with the announcement that only world-famous stars would appear in his features. [Laemmle is here referring to Adolph Zukor and his Famous Players in Famous Plays Company.]

So the man who had been paying in the neighborhood of $80 a week [actually $105 for the Universal program] for a service of one, two and three-reelers, found himself paying as much as $50 for a five-reeler for one day. When his moan of anguish at the lack of profits in his box office receipts reached the ears of the feature man, the latter calmed him by declaring that everything would be lovely just as soon as the public awoke to the fact that stars were appearing in pictures. Now, I'm not saying that stars won't bring business. They will. But how do you gain by the extra attendance, if the money it means is swallowed up in the cost of feature rentals?

One thing I know is this. The Universal Film Manufacturing Company has been turning out one, two and three-reel productions that, picture for picture, will stand comparison with the BEST five-reelers on the market. While feature organizations have been squandering money on stars who tomorrow may jump to a competing concern, we have been quietly laying plans to help our exhibitors earn the return on their investments to which they are entitled. There's room in the Universal fold for every showman who has got his bellyful of features, feature stars and their attending evils.

Mr. Zukor thought this rather unkind since it was Laemmle who started escalating salaries when he stole Florence Lawrence and Mary Pickford away from Biograph with huge salary increases.

In another blast, Laemmle (actually written by Cochrane) said,

The heart and soul, lungs and liver, backbone and stamina, brains and brawn of the moving picture business is THE SCIENTIFICALLY BALANCED PROGRAM.

The exhibitor who is building for the future ought to see by now that every time he indulges in so-called "features" he is spending his money for fluff that will never get him anywhere or anything.

A surprising thing about Laemmle's blasts against feature pictures is that the most famous picture Universal made between its origin in 1912 and the time Laemmle was writing had been a five-reel feature. This film, *Traffic in Souls*, was the company's biggest money-maker, grossing $450,000 on a $5,700 outlay.

The origin of this famous picture is clouded by tradition and myth. The traditional story is the one given by Terry Ramsaye in *A Million and One*

Nights. Bob Thomas repeats the same story in his book, *King Cohn.*

In 1913 New York had been rocked by two scandalous reports on white slavery. One was conducted by the Rockefeller Investigating Committee for the Suppression of Vice, headed by John D. Rockefeller, Jr. The other was the White Slavery Report of New York District Attorney Charles S. Whitman. The investigations showed that forced prostitution was the financial support of organized crime in the city. Girls were being compromised and even kidnapped off the streets

"Traffic in Souls"

A powerful, dramatic, full-blooded sermon, in which human emotions and adventures blend stirringly. Based on actual reports of the Rockefeller Investigating Committee, and the report of the District Attorney of New York City for the suppression of White Slavery.

Great Universal Drama in 6 parts

Jane Gail watches Howard Crampton pay off a politician to protect the White Slave operations exposed in *Traffic in Souls.* The picture got away with what, for the time, was raw sex because it was based upon police records.

George Loane Tucker, who had been with Universal since its IMP days, directed the company's first true hit, *Traffic in Souls.*

and literally kept as slaves in brothels owned by crime and political figures.

Several stage presentations were based upon these sensational disclosures. According to Ramsaye, George Loane Tucker saw one of these shows and was fired to make a similar movie. Tucker had been with Laemmle in the IMP days, but left with Ince to join Reliance. He remained with Reliance only a short time and then rejoined Universal as a director.

Ramsaye says Tucker approached Laemmle, who turned him down when Tucker said the picture would take five reels and cost five-thousand dollars Herbert Brenon, King Baggott, Jack Cohn, and Robert Daly, friends of Tucker, encouraged him to go ahead and make the film. Each of them promised to put up one-thousand dollars each to buy the film if Laemmle did not like it when it was finished. It was photographed a scene at a time "in odd moments when opportunity permitted, while keeping up with a continuous grind of one- and two-reel pictures."

After the picture was finished and before it was edited, Tucker quit to take a job in England. Cohn cut the picture. Laemmle did an about face and supported the picture against his angry board of directors. He knew he could not distribute it through the regular Universal Program and sold a one-third interest to Lee and Jake Shubert for thirty-three-thousand dollars. The Shuberts booked the film through their regular theaters.

So much for the oft-repeated legend. Tucker could not possibly have filmed a five-reel movie at odd moments in one month's time. His cameraman could not have checked out that much film from the camera supply department. He could always set up a camera at "odd moments," but he could not have gathered actors and actresses of the caliber of Ethel Grandin, Jane Gail, Howard Crampton, and Matt Moore anytime he had a few minutes to spare for a scene. Grandin and Gail were in special demand and not just working for Tucker. Their costumes would have had to be changed constantly and the sets could not have been broken down.

Knowing Laemmle's hatred of features, it seems incredible that his employees would have tried to put one by him. Laemmle had his peculiarities that increased as he got older, but in 1913 he had the reputation of being a very sharp businessman who kept a close eye on the balance sheets. Add to this the fact that there was no possible way that Universal could have distributed a five-reel film at that time.

As to a clue to what really happened, there is a statement attributed to Lee Shubert: "We were in *Traffic in Souls* from the beginning," and a statement by Walter McNamara, who wrote the scenario and is credited with being the producer, "It was my idea and I talked to the Shuberts about distributing it."

It seems apparent from this that the Shuberts agreed in advance to show the sex film in their theaters. In any event *Traffic in Souls* opened at the Shubert-owned Joe Weber's Theater on November 24, 1913, after a garish advertising campaign that promised to show "the traps cunningly laid for young girls by vice agents—Don't miss the most thrilling scene ever staged, the smashing of the Vice Trust!"

Traffic in Souls is the story of an honest cop named Officer Burke. Burke falls in love with the daughter of a man who was dismissed as useless by his company after becoming disabled. Matt Moore played Burke and Jane Gail was the girl, Mary Barton.

Mary has a flighty sister, Lorna (Ethel Grandin), who falls into the hands of the prostitution ring. Lorna is under the impression that she is to be given a chance to appear on the stage. Mary, learning what has happened, goes to Burke for help. Together they trap the vice ring head by recording his conversation on a new dictaphone that her crippled father has invented. The head of the vice ring is exposed as the leader of a Purity Group. Lorna learns her lesson. Mary and Officer Burke are married.

George Loane Tucker did a remarkable job in directing the picture, foreshadowing his later work in *The Miracle Man.* Rockefeller was quoted as saying the scenes in the brothels and the scenes where the kidnapped girls were beaten until they agreed to become prostitutes were exactly as witnesses had testified before his committee.

The picture threw censors off balance. It was a moral film and a great social document, for it showed intolerable social conditions exactly as they were. But the film still dealt with sex and therefore was something to be shunned. Before they could decide what to do, the film was showing in twenty-eight theaters in New York alone.

About one month after *Traffic in Souls* stunned the motion picture world, there was another shock when Selig presented the first true American motion picture serial. There had been serials made in Europe previous to this and in 1912 Edison made the series film, *What Happened to Mary,* which was timed to show at the same time as installments of the story ran in *Woman's World* magazine.

The film, *The Adventures of Kathlyn,* was devised as a newspaper circulation dodge. Walter Howey of the Chicago *Tribune* decided that it would help circulation of his paper if they ran a serial story tied to a serial movie. He discussed the plan with Max Annenberg, the paper's circulation manager, and got his approval. Annenberg then closed a deal with Selig to produce the film. Howey, the prototype of the tough editor, was the model for the editor in the famous Hecht-MacArthur play, *The Front Page.* Howey also helped D. W. Griffith fight censorship of *The Birth of a Nation* in Chicago. Griffith, grateful, asked if he could do something for Howey. "Well, I have a

niece, Kathleen Morrison, who wants to be an actress," Howey said. Griffith groaned, but gave the girl a contract. He did nothing for her career, but she persisted and eventually became Colleen Moore.

When *The Adventures of Kathlyn* was released in December 1913 with Kathlyn Williams and Tom Santschi in the leading roles, it took the movie public by storm and greatly boosted the *Tribune's* circulation. Immediately the movie industry hurried to jump on the bandwagon.

Universal was there with the rest, but not fast enough to be number two in the serial sweepstakes.

General Love (E. M. Keller) orders Lt. Gibson (Harry Shumm) under arrest after vital papers disappear. Lucille Love (Grace Cunard) is appalled in the 1914 serial, *Lucille Love, the Girl of Mystery.*

Edison released *Dolly of the Dailies* on January 31, 1914. Universal released *Lucille Love, the Girl of Mystery,* with Francis Ford and Grace Cunard, on April 4, 1914, just one week ahead of the first

Grace Cunard, her runabout forced off the road by the villainous Francis Ford, is injured in *Lucille Love,* Universal's first serial.

installment of Eclectic Films' *The Perils of Pauline.*

Isadore Bernstein, who was manager of the West Coast division of Universal, told Cunard and Ford that Laemmle had wired them to get started on a serial. Bernstein, who was a writer himself, suggested that they could move faster by taking one of their unreleased films and tacking a cliff-hanging ending on it and going on from there. Ford suggested a film they had just done about spies in the Philippines.

"A serial is going to have to cover a lot of ground," he said. "A spy background will let us go anywhere and do just about anything."

"Can you do it?" Bernstein asked Grace.

"Oh, sure," Miss Cunard replied with outward confidence. Her inward confidence must have been something else, for she usually proudly signed her scenarios. This time she wrote the script for Lucille Love under the pen name of "Master Pen."

The plot of *Lucille Love* revolved around the semisinister figure of the international spy Hugo Loubeque. Years before Hugo and General Sumpter Love had been rivals while cadets at West Point. This engendered a hatred of Love that Hugo, after he became a spy, never forgot.

As the film opens, General Love is in command in the Philippine Islands. He gives some plans to his aide, Lieutenant Gibson, to put away. Loubeque steals the plans, causing Gibson's arrest. Gibson is engaged to Love's daughter, Lucille, who sets out to recover the stolen material. Harry Schumm, a veteran of the Ford-Cunard two-reel series, played Gibson. Never before in anybody's picture has a hero—defining the word as one who gets the girl—had so little to do. He appears only in the first chapter when he permits the plans to be stolen and in the last when Lucille gets him freed.

The picture then settles into an international chase, seesawing back and forth as first Lucille and then Loubeque get the plans.

Among the first New York Motion Picture Company actors to join the new Universal were Grace Cunard and Francis Ford. The team, shown here in the 1912 one-reeler, *The White Vaquero*, were Big U's most popular stars during 1914 and 1915 when they lost out to J. Warren Kerrigan.

She is wrecked in an airplane, shanghaied aboard a ·ship, shipwrecked in the South Seas, washed up on an island peopled with beast men, rescued and taken to China, captured by Loubeque, imprisoned in Mexico, and then succeeds in getting the plans in San Francisco.

Throughout the picture Loubeque proves not to be the complete villain. He frequently saves Lucille from dangers in the course of their long struggle.

Ernest Shields, who had been making one-reel comedies for Universal, played a sinister butler who aided Loubeque.

The first returns on *Lucille Love* caused jubilation in the Universal business office. Isadore Bernstein, the West Coast manager, wired Laemmle, suggesting they immediately plan for a follow-up Ford-Cunard serial, and that they employ a top-rate writer to begin preparing the script immediately.

Laemmle agreed and Bernstein contacted Louis Joseph Vance, the famous author of the Lone Wolf stories. Vance agreed, provide he could retain book rights to the script.

The extraordinary success of *Lucille Love* established Grace Cunard and Francis Ford as Universal's top stars. Prior to this their one- and two-reelers had been popular, but not as much so as King Baggott and J. Warren Kerrigan films.

Both members of the team were veteran stage and screen actors before coming to Universal. Grace Cunard, officially, was born in Paris, France, of exotic parentage. Grace Cunard, actually, was born in Columbus, Ohio, of parents who were quite ordinary citizens. Her name was Harriet Mildred Jeffries and her birthdate was April 8, 1893. She made her stage debut at thirteen in a play called *Dora Thorne.* She then performed with a stock company and toured with Eddie Foy and his company.

When the Foy engagement ended at the close of 1909, Grace looked for work until the summer of 1910 when she gave up and applied for work with Biograph. Apparently she and Griffith did not get along well, for she moved to Lubin where she made a series of pictures in 1911. Ever on the lookout for something that would give her more control of her work, she left Lubin to join Kessel and Bauman's operations. Here, under the dictatorial Thomas H. Ince, she had even less to say about her work. Ince kept control even of the films he did not personally direct. He rewrote and approved all scripts. These were given to subordinate directors with orders to shoot *exactly* as the script was written.

While she was personally unhappy with her work for the New York Motion Picture Company, it turned out to be her big break, for she met a young actor-director named Francis Ford, who wasn't really "Francis Ford" at all. He was a Maine Yankee of Irish descent named Frank Feeney. He was gifted with a long, expressive face that could fit many types of roles. This got him employed with stock companies and eventually he hit Broadway as a stage manager.

According to a story John Ford, his brother, told Peter Bogdanovich, an actor billed as Francis Ford got drunk and was unable to appear one night. Young Feeney stepped into the role and was a hit. He continued to appear as "Francis Ford" for the remainder of the play's run. By that time he had made such a name for himself as Ford that he continued to use it.

Ford toured for some time with Fanny Davenport and when times got bad—like so many actors of the period—he condescended to take some film roles until things got better. This brought him eventually to the New York Motion Picture Company where he met Grace Cunard.

The two sparked from the first, but not romantically. Both were married to nonprofessionals and remained so. Artistically and professionally, they were a perfect match.

During the months they were with NYMP at Inceville, Grace kept a close watch on Francis Ford. She admired him as an actor and as a director. She had already begun writing her own scripts and she was seeking a partner for a future team of writer-actress and director-actor to form her own company.

The chance came when Bauman and Kessel withdrew from the newly formed Universal organization. Grace suggested to Ford that they form a team and approach Laemmle. Isadore Bernstein, the Universal West Coast Manager, talked with Henry McRae, Universal's Director-General, and okayed the proposition.

During the last months of 1912 and 1913, the pair established a reputation for turning out suspenseful, action pictures of every type. This climaxed in the *Lucille Love* serial, which established them as the top team at Universal.

At this time Universal was very strong on teams. Groups developed almost into stock companies with the same director, actor, actress, and supporting cast. Laemmle believed that if the public liked a certain girl and boy they would like them in another picture. Other teams who developed during this period were Phillips Smalley and Lois Weber, Pauline Bush and William Dowlan, Dorothy Phillips and William Stowell, Rosemary Theby and Hobart Henley, and Robert Z. Leonard and pretty Ella Hall, among others.

The early returns on *Lucille Love* were so gratifying that Laemmle ordered that the next serial start immediately so that it could be backed right against *Lucille Love.* He even suggested that the exchanges try to get exhibitors to show the final chapter of *Lucille Love* and the first chapter of the next serial at the same time. This, he suggested, would hook the audience on the new film.

This new policy eliminated Ford and Cunard, who were still working to complete *Lucille.* Wilfred Lucas was handed the Louis Joseph Vance original, *The Trey O'Hearts,* and told to get busy. Bess Meredith—who later fancied her name by spelling it Meredyth—was given the script to—as Louis Joseph Vance said—"mince into such scene-fodder as is more palatable to the reeling camera." Cleo Madison was given the double role of Judith and Rose, George Larkin was cast as the hero Alan, and Edward Sloman—later a director—was the villain Seneca Trine.

As to the story itself, the author's opinion of it was set forth in a preface to the book version, published in 1914: "The work between these covers, however grave its many faults and short-comings, was penned with a single aim, to wit, to compose a story susceptible to adaption to motion-picture purposes. Its brazen impudent in respect to probability was demanded by the fact that each episode of the fifteen here presented must of necessity embrace sufficient moving incident to warrant some two thousand feet of film."

From all accounts, the heroine, Cleo Madison, must have been a prototype for today's most ardent women's libbers.

She told a *Photoplay* magazine interviewer: "Men are going to have to get over the fool idea that women have no brains and quit getting insulted at the thought that a skirt-wearer can do their work as well as they can."

As a teenager, she suddenly decided she would be an actress. Her prudish family was horrified. So she walked out to join a stock company. Before long she was manager. Then like so many others, bad business drove her into the movies. She loved the work, but after being her own manager in stock, she resented directors telling her what to do. She kept egging Isadore Bernstein to let her direct her own pictures. After completing the *Trey O'Hearts,* she became temperamental and found continual fault with her directors. Finally Bernstein gave way and let her direct her films. They were not successful.

The Trey O'Hearts was the story of twin sisters, Judith and Rose Trine. Their vicious, crippled father, played by Edward Sloman, blamed the dead

Cleo Madison battles Injun Joe Garcia in the 1914 serial, *The Trey of Hearts*. While a money-maker, the serial did not achieve the popularity of *Lucille Love*.

different. And so, presumably, the villainess and the hero lived happily ever after while the heroine died.

In these beginning years serials were not exclusively kid's Saturday matinee fare as they later became. They were adult films, and programmed accordingly. An exhibitor who brought individual films, of course, could schedule the serials whenever he pleased, but subscribers to the Universal Program got *Lucille Love* on Tuesdays along with a split reel and a comedy.

Before Lucille ran its twenty-two chapters, Bernstein started a third serial. This was *The Master Key*, a story by John Fleming Wilson. It was directed by Robert Z. Leonard who later directed a number of Mae Murray films. His co-star was pretty Ella Hall.

Leonard graduated from the University of Colorado and immediately went to work in a Denver theater as a singer. His fine baritone voice led him into comic opera. In one touring company in which he sang, Lon Chaney was a male dancer and Anna Little (later another Universal actress) played feminine leads. Selig saw Leonard during a West Coast performance and persuaded the young man to join the Selig Polyscope Company, the first movie company to film on the West Coast. Leonard left Selig to join Universal where he teamed with Ella Hall in a series of shorts.

Ella was a fragile, dolllike creature who had been on the stage since she was a small child, debuting in *The Grand Army Man* for David Belasco. Later she understudied Mary Pickford in *The Warrens of Virginia*. This was not rewarding, for Mary Pickford never missed a performance. When she couldn't find another part, Ella applied for work at Biograph, where she spent two years with D. W. Griffith. She left Biograph to work with James Kirkwood at Reliance and then worked for a few months with Kinemacolor, the first serious attempt to make motion pictures in direct color. When this project collapsed, Fred Balshofer sent her to Ince at 101-Bison. Lois Weber and her husband Phillips Smalley took a liking to her and brought Ella to Universal. In an interview in *Moving Picture Stories Magazine* in 1915, Ella said, "If it hadn't been for Miss Weber's kindness and patience when things seemed most difficult for me, I really don't think I should be where I am today."

From the Webers, she joined Leonard, which led to her part in the third Universal serial, *The Master Key*.

father of hero Alan Law (George Larkin) for his affliction. Trine intended to kill Alan. Trine's twin daughters were exactly opposite in character. Judith was vicious like her father and Rose, who loved Alan Law, was sweet and gentle. They were so identical that even Alan Law, who loved Rose, could not tell them apart.

The trey of hearts from which the picture took its name is a "death card" which Trine kept sending to Law as part of his war of nerves.

Judith, who mortally hates her sister Rose, helps her father in his scheme to kill Law. In the course of this she becomes regenerated and falls in love with Law herself.

Then in one of the most peculiar endings of any film, Law is married to Rose. Just after the ceremony a bolt of lightning strikes the chapel. Rose is killed and Law is injured. When Law recovers he finds Judith nursing him. He thinks it is his wife, Rose. Judith did not tell him any

Another 1914 serial was *The Master Key* with Robert Z. Leonard doubling as star and director. Tiny Ella Hall, who supported Leonard in several two-reelers, was the co-star.

A very rare still from an early Lon Chaney Universal film shows William C. Dowlan (as Bashful Bill) and Chaney (as the Greaser) in Allan Dwan's two-reel *The Tragedy of Whispering Creek*, released under the 101-Bison Brand on May 2, 1914.

"THE PURSUIT OF HATE"

Dick La Reno, Lois Weber, Phillips Smalley, and Ella Hall in *The Pursuit of Hate*. The Smalleys liked tiny Ella and helped establish her at Universal.

The story involved a mine owned by Ella Hall and the efforts of her superintendent, Robert Leonard, to prevent it being stolen from her by enemies of her dead father. Mixed in with the plot was a hidden treasure of her father's whose secret lay in *The Master Key*.

At the conclusion of *Lucille Love,* Grace Cunard was completely worn out. Laemmle graciously stood the bill for a vacation trip to Hawaii for the entire Ford-Cunard company for their fine work on the serial—but with the understanding they would take a camera along and begin filming a two-reel series while they were there. This developed into the *My Lady Raffles* series. Grace Cunard played the female leader of a gang of crooks and Francis Ford was the detective who almost, but not quite, got her in each installment. Grace conceived the idea as a serial, but with the *Trey O'Hearts* showing, *The Master Key* ready for release, and famous mystery novelist E. Phillips

Oppenheim writing *The Black Box* for early 1915 production, Laemmle had all the serials he could absorb for the moment. He wanted program fillers and lots of them, but he promised Ford and Cunard that they could make the serial to follow *The Black Box.*

Part of the reason for delaying the next Cunard-Ford serial was information from the accounting department that the team's two-reelers released early in 1914 before they went to work on *Lucille Love* had proven exceptionally good money-makers. They were among the best films the two had made.

One released February 3, 1914, was a Civil War drama, *In the Fall of '64.* A Confederate ball is interrupted by the arrival of Union soldiers. Captain Ford rushes out to battle. The enemy capture the estate of Virginia (Grace Cunard), Captain Ford's sweetheart. Ford is later captured spying behind Union lines. Virginia, disguised as an idiotic boy, upsets a candle to plunge the room into darkness. This permits Ford to escape. The

Nabbed, a 1915 two-reeler, was from the long-running *My Lady Raffles* series of Grace Cunard and Francis Ford.

42

Union officer penetrates Virginia's masquerade, but she escapes to the Confederate line with secret information that permits Ford to win the battle.

Another release on February 10, 1914, was the three-reeler, *The Bride of Mystery.* This was a Ford-Cunard version of *Trilby,* changed sufficiently to escape plagiarism. Ford, a famous

In another murder and theft in which the hypnotist is involved, Countess X is apparently killed. Through his great skill Ford revives her and when she is freed of the hypnotic influence, they are married. Sometime later the hypnotist returns and hypnotically forces Countess X to accompany him. Ford rushes to rescue her and the villain floods a

Grace Cunard, disguised as a half-wit, overturns a candle to permit her brave hero, Confederate officer Francis Ford, to escape from Yankee soldiers in *In the Fall of '64,* made in 1914.

doctor, is enchanted by a strange actress who seems in a trance. Then he notices a man in the audience watching her with a peculiar penetrating stare. This man, a murderer and thief, has hypnotic power over the girl, who is known as Countess X.

subterranean passage to drown them. They escape but the hypnotist is killed.

Their biggest hit was *The Twins' Double,* released March 10, 1914. This film was conceived when Grace Cunard said she would like to play a

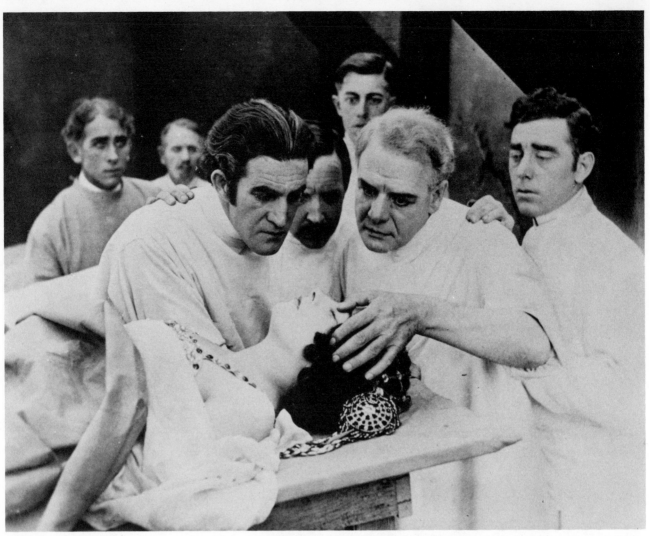

In *The Bride of Mystery* Grace Cunard wrote a role for herself based upon the basic idea of *Trilby,* in which she is rescued from the clutches of a Svengali character by a noble doctor played by Francis Ford, who also directed the three-reeler.

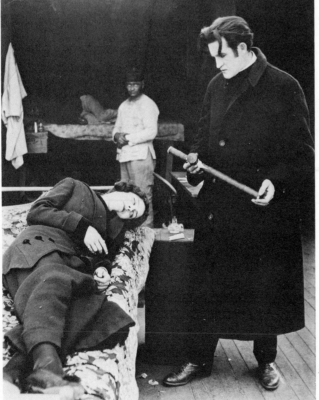

Grace Cunard took a triple part in the 1914 film, *The Twins' Double.* She played twin sisters and an evil woman who looked exactly like them. Here a saddened Francis Ford finds his sweetheart, one of the twins, in an opium den.

44

dual role. Ford objected. He said the double exposure necessary to make one person look like two involved too much time. Earlier, when double exposures were novelties, it was worth the trouble, but not any more.

Grace, reluctant to drop the idea, came up with a new suggestion—a triple exposure. She would appear as three identical women in the same film. That had never been done before. She outlined a plot idea she called *The Twins' Double.*

In the story Nell and Jo are identical twins. Nell, who is loved by Detective Phil Kelly (Francis Ford), goes to an opium den for a thrill. Grace, a crook, finds her there and is startled to discover that she and Nell look alike. Grace searches the drugged woman's purse, finding a note saying the two sisters are going to a masquerade party that night. Grace, intending to pull a robbery, goes to the party as Nell. Neither Jo nor Kelly realizes that she is not Nell.

Grace steals a society matron's diamond necklace. At this moment, Nell—recovering from her drugged stupor—arrives at the party. Kelly, seeing the three women in the room, realizes that the twins have a double. Grace escapes and goes to the opium den. Nell also goes there for more drugs. Kelly arrives to find Nell asleep with an opium pipe in her hand. He at first thinks that she is Grace, but discovers the truth in time to capture the female crook. Nell, contrite, promises to give up drugs.

The scene in which all three images of Grace Cunard appear at the same time was very skillfully done and highly praised at the time. The work was done by cameraman Al Siegler, who had worked with Vitagraph as an assistant cameraman and then one year with Universal as a cameraman.

The triple exposure work in *The Twins' Double* was so popular that Ford and Cunard repeated the gimmick in *The Return of the Twins' Double,* also a 1914 Gold Seal Release.

The Twins's Double was such a hit that the basic idea was repeated in another film called *The Return of the Twins' Double.*

45

5 Picture City

The Golden Year for Universal in the silent era was 1915. The trust was finally dissolved. Universal was making big money, far more than Zukor and Lasky with their features. It stars were tops in popularity. And most important of all, Laemmle opened Universal City.

Universal City—a town devoted to motion pictures—was born when Carl Laemmle asked Bill Swanson to find a site where Universal could build a bigger and better equivalent of Inceville. Uncle Carl wanted a place where he could consolidate all his production, including eventually closing down East Coast filming.

Swanson found a chicken ranch about ten miles from Los Angeles and three miles from Hollywood. Swanson asked several friends to look the place over. Everyone condemned the place. It was hilly, covered with rocks and trees, and cut by a stream. The only way to get to the place was along a dirt road that became impassable in wet weather.

Surprisingly, when Laemmle came out a month later he was delighted with the location and gave orders to buy the entire 250 acres. This was in late 1912. Work began in 1913 to improve the place and build a paved road into the ranch. Turning the rocks and hills into the "first municipality dedicated to making motion pictures" was entrusted to William "Big Bill" Horsley, brother of David Horsley of Nestor Company.

Laemmle could legitimately call his the "first municipality" because Inceville was merely an outdoor studio. Universal City was designed to be a town as well as a studio. Along with prop warehouses, film laboratories, dressing rooms, rows of outdoor stages, an indoor studio lighted with Cooper Hewitt tubes, a zoo, stables, and other purely picture related structures, he also constructed a fire station, a police station and a city hall.

An advance publicity story about the police station sounded a little embarrassed. It said, "Mounted on the best steeds from the Universal paddocks, they may be seen riding slowly about the streets of the city, covering their beats and keeping a wary eye open for possible speeders who feel inclined to take advantage of the unexcelled boulevards and disregard the fifteen mile an hour signs that are placed on either side of them.

"While as a matter of fact, there is little need for a police squad to keep order in Universal City, if the occasion should arise when they are needed, they would be needed at once. And it is for that possible emergency that the Universal has employed them."

March 15, 1915, was the official opening day for Universal City, but production began earlier at the new plant. A number of films were completed there before March 15. *Damon and Pythias,* with Herbert Rawlinson and William Worthington as the steadfast Greek friends, was the first film completed at Universal City.

Each department moved into its new quarters as

46

The main entrance of Universal City as it looked in 1914
just before the official opening in March 1915.

Sometimes behind the scenes was funnier than what got on
the screen. An example is this shot of James Horne, at left,
rehearsing an L-KO comedy with Gale Henry in 1915.
While prop men on the scaffolding drop paper "snow," the
three pursuing Gale and her boyfriend slip on the ice. A
painted backdrop makes the background.

William Worthington dropped his director's role to play the Senator with Herbert Rawlinson in *Damon and Pythias,* the legendary Greek friends, in the first movie completed at the new Universal City. Otis Turner directed.

they were finished by Horsley's crews. This gradual shift from Edendale and other locations permitted the move to be made without losing a single day's shooting. About fifty films were made in Universal City before the place officially opened. The company kept very little backlog and needed a minimum of five reels a week of assorted subjects to meet exchange demands.

Among the films finished at Universal City was the Ford-Cunard two-reeler made partly on the Malibu coast, *Smuggler's Island.*

In this hastily made picture, Grace and Francis were sweethearts. Appearing as they did almost once a week, their relations must have become confusing to their fans. One week they were sweethearts. The next she was a crook and he was a detective. Then the following week, she was the heroine and he was the villain. Then again she might be his daughter, as in he 1914 *Ghost of Smiling Jim.* Once she was a serving maid in a tavern and he was George Washington.

In *Smuggler's Island* Grace snubs Ford for flirting with other girls and walks off to make eyes herself at a Coast Guard officer who later is captured by smugglers he surprises on the beach.

Grace, a witness to the capture, is abducted by the smuggler chief, Harry Schumm. Ford sees what has happened, but is too late to stop it. He rushes to the Coast Guard headquarters, but no one will listen. He forces them with a gun to accompany him in their boat. They overtake the smugglers, because Grace has stolen a gun with a single bullet and shot out the engine. By the time the rescuers get aboard, Grace had fought with and knocked out Schumm. She and Ford are reunited happily.

Cleo Madison, finishing work in the *Trey O'Hearts,* was rushed into *The Mystery Woman,* directed by Wilfred Lucas and released January 30, 1915. Bess Meredyth wrote the script. Joe King was the hero and Edward Sloman was the villain.

Cleo and Joe had just been married and he presented her with the deed to his rich mine. Sloman, trying to steal the deed, attacks them. Joe is left for dead and Cleo is turned into an idiot by a bullet that grazes her head during the fight.

She wanders off to another mining town where she lives in a haunted house and has the reputation of being a crazy woman. Sloman, who fled after supposedly killing Cleo's husband, discovers her and realizes that she may still have the deed to the mine. He attacks her, but Cleo escapes. He pursues her. In the meantime, her husband, Joe, has recovered and learns where his wife is. He arrives just as Sloman catches her again. They fight. Cleo, knocked down, regains her memory from the blow on her head. She grabs Sloman's gunhand as he tries to shoot Joe. The bullet goes into Sloman instead. Joe and Cleo live happily ever after.

With such films as these thrown at her, it is small wonder that Miss Madison thought she could do better making her own movies.

However, King Baggott had his best film since he made *Ivanhoe,* with Herbert Brenon directing, in England in 1913. It was called *The Millionaire Engineer* and was directed by Baggott at the IMP studio at Ft. Lee, New Jersey.

Grace Cunard struggles with smuggler chief Harry Shumm
in the 1915 two-reeler *Smuggler Island.*

Their Hour, a domestic drama, had Cleo Madison and
Wilfred Lucas heading the cast. Zoe Beck and Buster
Emmons (Edmonds) are the children.

49

Baggott is shown as a self-made millionaire railroad tycoon. He is having a party to announce his engagement to Arline Pretty, who also played with him in the recent *An Oriental Romance.* Some of his workers, resenting their starvation wages while he has parties, rush the door to lay their grievances before him. He refuses to talk to them and Arline, who sympathizes with the men, gives him back his ring.

Arline Pretty plays the society girl who fell in love with a "high caste" Chinese boy, King Baggott. Frank Smith plays the Chinese father. *An Oriental Romance* was released in 1915 and directed by George A Lessey.

Shortly after a forest fire starts and threatens an orphanage. For some reason, the only way to get them out is to run a train through the blaze. None of the engineers will risk the run. So Baggott drives the engine himself, plunging through the flames to rescue the poor kids, with only Arline to help him. During the ordeal, he comes to realize the justice of the striker's demands and accedes to them on his return. They hail him as a true hero and so does Arline.

The picture was praised for its realistic fire scenes. This was as it should have been, for Baggott spent a lot of money on them. He had five shacks built along the railroad right of way. The interiors were stuffed with trash and reels of old nitrate film, which burns explosively. Leaves were piled on the railroad track and also set afire. When the fire was blazing well, the engine charged through the smoke and flame.

Baggott claimed he actually drove the engine for the fire run. A regular engineer named Tom Mcguire spent two days teaching him how to handle the throttle. Then Mcguire crouched in the engine cabin out of sight so he could take over if Baggott got into any trouble.

Some other pictures of this season were Joseph de Grasse's *The Measure of a Man* with Pauline Bush, William Dowlan, and Lon Chaney. It was the story of a gambler who tries to sacrifice for what he believes is his wife's sake only to learn that she loves him after all.

He Fell in Love With His Mother-in-law, a one-reel Joker comedy release January 30, 1915, showed that Universal comedies frequently had better knit plots than the so-called dramas. In this one, which was really funny, William Franey—a Chaplin type—is married to slovenly Gale Henry. Gale makes her husband mend his own clothes, clean the house, and wash the dishes. Then one day as Gale is threatening Franey with a rolling pin, her mother arrives for a visit.

The audience expects—and so does Franey—the typical mother-in-law, but in a switch Mom sides with the henpecked husband. She sets about putting her daughter in her place. She does such a good job that the grateful husband brings his mother-in-law a box of candy and a big bouquet of roses. Gale stands watching them with a sad expression.

J. Warren Kerrigan started a new Terrence O'Rourke series. He supplanted King Baggott as Big U's most popular male star and rivaled those of any other studio.

Ben Wilson starred and directed *Children of Chance.* The feminine lead in this story of mixed-up babies who grow up to marry was taken by Dorothy Phillips, who married Allan Holubar, the Big U director. Miss Phillips was a lovely, dark-eyed, dark-haired girl of twenty-three—somewhat older than the teenagers Universal preferred. The lenses of the day accentuated skin wrinkles, lines, and imperfections and young girls were preferred, since the camera added years to a woman's face.

Dorothy was born in Baltimore, Maryland, in 1892. She appeared on the stage before joining Essanay. After two years with this company, she moved to Universal to work her way through comedies to two-reel drama. She did not attract a lot of attention in these, but was only two years away from her big triumph in *Hell Morgan's Girl.*

A British officer, played by Francis Ford, is captured and dragged before the queen of *The Hidden City,* Grace Cunard. A 101-Bison film made in 1915.

Other films included Frank Lloyd, later the famous director, in *The Last Serenade;* Billie Ritchie and Pathe Lehrman in *After Her Millions;* Mary Fuller in *His Guardian Angel;* Eddie Lyons and Victoria Forde (the future Mrs. Tom Mix) in *Jed's Little Elopement;* and one of the real future greats, director John Ford, in a supporting role in *Three Bad Men and a Girl,* starring his brother Francis and Grace Cunard.

Jack Ford graduated from high school in Portland, Maine, in 1913, and immediately joined his older brother, Francis, in California. Ford always claimed he started as an assistant prop man, but old stills, such as *The Battle of Bull Run,* 1913, shows that he was playing bit parts from the beginning. He also doubled for Francis in some films, notably, *Lucille Love.* From these supporting roles, he moved into leads. Some of the old reviews credit him with considerable riding ability in his westerns.

He didn't have a matinee idol's looks, unfortunately, and gradually moved into direction where his best Universal films were made with western star Harry Carey, a banker's son who became the best exponent of the West after William S. Hart.

Three Bad Men and a Girl was among the best of the Ford-Cunard two-reelers. It was a western comedy-drama. And being played for laughs, the inconsistencies and coincidences that played such large parts in Grace Cunard's scripts were not objectional.

Said one review: *"Three Bad Men and a Girl* is one of those gallavantin' comedies that simply makes one howl from initial flash to censorship tag. The whole play is an exceedingly clever satire on the more or less impossible Western dramas which now have about finished their vogue.

"Seventeen cowboys jump to the backs of their horses at one and the same time, revolver shots are exchanged at point blank range every three

Francis Ford, with Grace Cunard and his brother Jack Ford—visible just behind the arm holding Francis' gun hand—were the principals in the 1915 two-reeler *Three Bad Men and a Girl.*

seconds, doors are broken in, and Grace Cunard escapes on a clothes line over a chasm umpty-steen feet deep, while Mexicans and Indians throw straight-from-the shoulder dingbats, inbings, eceybetoes and other unmentionable things at her. . . ."

The plot spins around three outlaws who hold up a stage on which Grace (Grace Cunard) is a passenger. A reward is posted for the bandits, but the only description is that two are tall and one short. Later when Joe (Francis Ford), Jim (Jack Ford), and Shorty (Major Paleolagus) ride into town they are mistaken for the three bad men.

Grace claims they are not the bandits, but the sheriff has the three disarmed and run out of town anyway. Later the unarmed trio discover the real bandits and capture them despite a lack of arms. By this time Mexicans have captured poor Grace. Joe, who has grown to admire the girl (love ripened fast in Big U's two-reelers, for there wasn't much

time), leads his two companions to the rescue and a fight to end all fights closes out the reel.

Since the end of 1914 Universal had been running ads inviting the public to visit Universal City for the official grand opening on March 15. One such ad showed three small cuts from the J. Warren Kerrigan series, *Terence O'Rouke,* above a large headline, "COME ON OUT TO UNIVERSAL CITY—WATCH US MAKING MOVIES."

> Dear Movie Fans:
> You will enjoy the greatest experience of your life if you will become the Universal's guest for a day at Universal City, Cal., when you attend the Panama-Pacific Exposition.
> Come to Universal City at our expense from San Francisco, on the occasion of the official opening of the Million Dollar Moving Picture City, the largest film studios in the world, March 15, 1915.
> The three big scenes in the little pictures above were staged in Universal City. That shows you some of the wonderful things you will see there. There are a thousand more wonderful things to be seen, for in this strangest city in the world the entire population is engaged in making moving pictures
> There is a stage 500 feet long. There is a world's wonder zoo. There is a police force, a fire department, public restaurant, hospital, cowboy and cavalry troop barracks, horses by the hundreds. You must not miss this.
> This is my cordial personal invitation to all movie fans to be my guest.
> Cordially Yours,
> Carl Laemmle, President.

Universal had already made a tie-in with the Panama-Pacific Exposition in San Francisco to be the official motion picture company for the celebration, permitting Universal to have an exclusive franchise to open movie houses on the exposition grounds. Now Laemmle made a deal with the railroads that they would include a side trip to Los Angeles at no extra cost for visitors coming to San Francisco for the fair. This enabled Universal to invite the public going to the exposition to come on down and see the New Universal City open on March 15.

This ad was aimed at the movie public. Laemmle was equally anxious that exhibitors come see his new plant as well. In *Universal Weekly,* a trade paper printed for Universal by the Motion Picture Newspaper Publishing Company (a Laemmle subsidiary), published in January this appeal from Laemmle:

Aw, C'mon Out!
Well, what are you going to do about it?

Are you going to come on out to Universal City on March 15th or not? Are you going to give old Dull Care a kick in the shins, drop your worries for a time and have some interesting fun, or are you going to stick around the old place and look glum?

Are you going to give your wife and kids a treat by bringing them to the "wonder city of the world" or not?

Just think of what it would mean to them and YOURSELF to see the inside workings of the biggest moving picture plant in the wide, wide world—a whole city where everybody is engaged in the making of motion pictures—a fairyland where the craziest things in the world happen—a place to think about and talk about all the rest of your days!

See how slapstick comedies are made. See how big serials are produced. See how your favorite screen stars do their work. See how the property men get everything in readiness for the cameraman to shoot. See how the scenic artists put old Dame Nature to shame. See the cowboys, Indians and soldiers at their best or worst.

See how we blow up bridges, burn down houses, wreck automobiles, and smash up things in general in order to give people of the world the kind of pictures they demand. See how buildings have to be erected just for a few scenes of one picture and then have to be torn down to make room for something else. See how we have to use the brains God gave us in every conceivable way in order TO MAKE THE PEOPLE LAUGH OR CRY OR SIT ON THE EDGE OF THEIR CHAIRS THE WORLD OVER!

The officers of the Universal will be there with bells on. If things are not lively enough to suit them, they'll get up some home-made vaudeville of their own or do something to inject a wad of pepper in the proceedings.

The managers of all Universal exchanges will be there. We want them to meet you [the exhibitors] and we want you to meet them. We want to prove to you that they don't wear horns, and we want to make them admit that you don't run around with a dagger up your sleeve.

C'mon out! Aw, c'mon!

The last movement of people and equipment to Universal City was completed at the end of February, although it took "Clara" to get the job done. Clara, a two-ton female elephant from the Big U zoo, was pressed into service by Bill Horsley to push truck and wagons that became mired in the mud during the February rains.

Once the move was completed, Laemmle came out with Cochrane from New York and a special inspection ball was held on March 7. Los Angeles business and civic officials were Big U's guests for the occasion.

And on the great day Universal City officially opened with a bang. Two hundred thousand people—the publicity department swore—jammed the city of pictures.

The festivities opened when actress Laura Oakley, as Universal City's police chief, presented Carl Laemmle with a golden key to the place. Then accompanied by Mayor Herbert Rawlinson as guide, Laemmle and his guests toured the new facilities.

Every Universal actor not actually sick in bed had orders to be there—and they were there. They acted as guides and ushers, as stunt men and as actors performing before empty cameras in scene setups to show visitors how motion pictures were made. As the climax of the opening show, the 101-Bison company of Indians and Cowboys staged a rip-roaring rodeo and Wild West show.

Describing the facilities, *Moving Picture World,* was struck by the completeness. After enumerating the expected buildings, the magazine reporter was awed to find an arsenal, a blacksmith shop, and even a bunkhouse for the cowboys who tended the stock.

"All over the place are sets, elaborate, some temporary and some that may well be permanent, that have been erected from time to time for large productions, ranging from castle walls to city streets," the reporter said.

"The Universal is building an experimental roof over a ten-foot section of its stage. It is to be of steel frame construction. It will be covered with galvanized steel, designed to roll back over the roof of the property building in the daytime. In the event of bad weather it will remain in position, and with the installation of lights have the full effect of an inside studio. The roof is designed primarily to prevent the striking of sets with which a director may not be finished at the close of a day when atmospheric conditions indicate rain. It is an experiment, but it looks good."

The open invitation to visitors for the grand opening went over so well that Laemmle, at Cochrane's suggestion, gave orders to H. O. Davis, who had succeeded Isadore Bernstein as general studio manager, to make studio tours a permanent feature. Cochrane thought it would be splendid advertising.

"It will cost us for guides and we'll have to pay actors and cameramen to put on shows for them, but if we charge a quarter we'll get our money back and get a million dollars worth of advertising for our trouble," he said.

This, the forerunner to today's great Southern California tourist attraction, the Universal Studio Tour, was a huge success, drawing four to five hundred visitors a day. This was despite the fact that special tourist cars from Los Angeles cost fifty cents for the round trip or just twice the price of admission. Cheapskates could use trolleys to Hollywood and then take a bus and make the round trip for thirty cents, which still made it cost more just to get there than it did to get in. The tours continued until rising production costs and distractions caused by tourists made for too many costly interruptions.

The only Universal activity outside Universal City were some productions still carried on in New York and at Ft. Lee, New Jersey, and the Lehrman L-KO operations, which continued to occupy the old Nestor studio at Sunset and Gower in Hollywood. Three companies were operating, turning out three one-reel comedies a week. The directors, in addition to Lehrman, were John G. Blystone and Harry Edwards.

The directorial staff at Universal City at this time consisted of Sidney Ayres, Al Christie, Allen Curtis, Horace Davey, Joseph de Grasse, William C. Dowlan, Francis Ford, Charles Giblyn, Jacques Jaccard, Burton King, Robert Z. Leonard, Frank Lloyd, O.A.C. Lund, Murdock MacQuarrie, Henry McRae, Phillips Smalley and Lois Weber, Otis Turner, and William Worthington.

The year 1915, although a great year for Universal as a leader of the motion picture industry, was not a good year financially for the industry as a whole. The European war had cut down on foreign sales of film. Also domestic prices were increasing across the board. At the same time the cost of production was in an inflation spiral.

The producers weren't really suffering. It was just that profits, which sometimes had ranged as high as one-thousand percent on films, had dropped so badly that in some cases producers were hard put to make one-hundred to two-hundred percent on their money.

Laemmle, always the leader in those days, continued to set the business pace for the industry. Just as he had led the industry in the fight against trust restrictions and against the "evils" of feature pictures (a battle he lost), he now took on the problem of reduced profits. He got little credit for this from rival producers. They observed sourly that the industry wouldn't be in a profit pinch if Laemmle hadn't invented the star system by paying Mary Pickford almost double what she had been getting from Biograph and then adding to her ego and unconscionable demands by giving her billing.

The only way to bring in more cash was to up the price of films to exhibitors. Universal was already charging more for its complete weekly program than any company except those devoted exclusively to features. It was not possible to raise exhibitor prices—unless exhibitors raised their own prices. The question was: would the moviegoing public pay it? Films were no longer a novelty and general attendance had not been growing as much as it had in the previous years, although serials were giving attendance a shot in the arm.

Laemmle's solution was a blast of advertising (paid for by the exhibitors, naturally) to convince the public that they should pay more at the box office. If advertising could convince people to buy clothing they didn't really need, as he had seen happen in his Oshkosh store, then it could convince them that they would get better pictures on the screen if they would just pay a nickel more at the box office.

In a broadside to the trade, Laemmle wrote:

MR. EXHIBITOR: You've got to raise your admission price sooner or later; These ads will help you do it quickly and successfully.

There is no more reason for your selling admissions for less than they are worth than there is for your neighbor, the grocer, selling butter for 25¢ a pound that costs him 26¢.

If you let the public think you are increasing prices just to get the extra nickels to pay for a new automobile—they may pass you up.

If you show the people that with the U program THEY ALWAYS get their money's worth, no matter what price you charge, if you show them that you are giving them more for their money than is reasonable—if you tell the truth—show them the bare facts as we do in these ad cuts—they'll be with you to a man. You can raise your prices—put and keep your house up to a top-notch standard, and they'll thank you for it.

No moving picture concern in the country is constantly plugging for its exhibitors—365 days in the years, the way the Universal has done, is doing and will continue to do.

This plan will raise your prices for you—it will work while you sleep—if you'll start it going—but it can't do anything for you until you get the cuts, run them in your newspaper—use them as they were intended to be used.

We've done our share—now IT IS UP TO YOU.

The ad series consisted of four prepared mats. The first said:

MOVIE FANS! You see 3 times as many reels today as you did 5 years ago for the same old price. STOP AND CONSIDER. Five years ago the average Moving Picture Theater showed only from 2 to 10 reels of pictures a week. TODAY the average Picture Theater shows anywhere from 20 to 30 reels per week.

Have you ever stopped to realize that everybody that has anything to do with moving pictures has been spending MORE MONEY except YOU who attend moving pictures shows at the same old price?

These ads went on for four issues, with Laemmle suggesting that the exhibitor run each one for three days. The final one was headed:

"THE PUBLIC HAS DECIDED IN ITS OWN FAVOR,"

and then on to say that the majority was glad to pay more to get quality movies. The public must have been surprised to learn that it had agreed to the price raise, but they paid.

Frank MacQuarrie escapes through a secret door in the cellar while villainous William Worthington detracts Herbert Rawlinson, the great "Sanford Quest" in E. Phillips Oppenheim's *The Black Box,* a serial hit of 1915.

It didn't take the public long to find out where the extra money was going. Laemmle broke out the biggest type to inform the world that he had paid famed mystery novelist E. Phillips Oppenheim ten thousand dollars for the original script, *The Black Box.* In one ad Universal bragged:

We went over to London recently and slipped E. Phillips Oppenheim ten thousand green boys to write our next serial. He did so and called it, "The Black Box." It slips on the screen March 8. Oppenheim loves to tie the hero in a knot and watch him dig his way out. Yes, and he's always chucking things in the hero's way. By the time Eee Pee's hero reaches the finish, he's tired enough to retire. You've simply got to see "The Black Box." Go around to your favorite theater and tell the manager to book the thrilling thing.
TEN THOUSAND GREEN LADS! Think of it. Have you thought of it? All right. It shows you how far the UNIVERSAL will go to entertain the people of this country. It's the greatest film manufacturing concern in the world.

Universal had had some close shaves with its previous serial. Exhibition had been started before the film was completely shot. As a result there was often times when no one was sure that the next installment would reach the screen in time. In one case negatives shot in San Francisco were misdirected and did not reach the processing laboratory on schedule. In another the death of an extra brought a police investigation that delayed production two days before the coroner was satisfied that it was an accident. Camera trouble also contributed to difficulties.

With all this in mind, Laemmle gave orders that *The Black Box* would not be released until the final chapter was in the can. H. O. Davis, the studio manager, wasn't happy about this. His success depended upon how much money the studio made. When he authorized money to be spent on a film, it made his balance sheet look better if this money was returned—with a profit—as quickly as possible. Film sitting in cans represented money spent that was not earning a dime.

Davis, a tall man who towered over diminutive Carl Laemmle like Mutt over Jeff, was efficient and well liked where money wasn't involved. The very mention of money seemed to change his personality. For example, he is supposed to have told Laemmle that Lon Chaney, an up and coming support actor in 1915, was one of the best actors on the lot. But when Chaney hit him up for a raise Davis screamed like Chaney had asked for the studio manager's left arm. "Why should I pay you more?" he asked. "You're just another damned actor!" According to a story often repeated, Chaney was so annoyed at being refused the ten dollars raise that when he returned to make the great *Hunchback of Notre Dame* he demanded an extra ten dollars above the offered contract price to make up for the raise he'd asked Davis for eight years before.

All the legends about mismanagement and nepotism at Universal belong to a later period. Under H. O. Davis each director was given a budget, and if he wished to remain at Big U, he could jolly well bring the picture in on or under budget or else.

6 A Flood of Pictures

In Laemmle's business philosophy greatness meant bigness. Already he had the biggest plant, the largest number of employees, and the largest turnout of products of any competitor. But that wasn't enough. He was on the lookout for more.

For some time the company was known to employees and exhibitors as Big U. The nickname came from some ads the publicity department had prepared in which the heads of different stars were inserted inside a huge initial U. After the name gained currency, Laemmle organized another production company and named it Big U. So by the beginning of 1915 the production units included 101-Bison, L-KO comedies, Joker comedies, Victor, Sterling, Rex, Powers, Nestor, Animated Weekly, Eclair, Gold Seal, IMP, and the new Big U.

In 1915 Laemmle suddenly sprang another surprise. After loudly condemning feature pictures longer than three-reels, he launched Broadway Features, which was a direct copy of Adolph Zukor's Famous Players idea. Just why Laemmle suddenly decided to make features while he continued to write editorials in *Universal Weekly* condemning them and prophecying that feature producers would go broke is not clear. Apparently he was irritated because Jesse L. Lasky had gotten a ream of publicity after he had scooped the industry by signing Geraldine Farrar, the most popular prima donna of her day. Despite the fact that opera stars seemed poor material for the silent drama, DeMille had gotten an excellent performance out of her in *Maria Rosa*, and *Carmen* was

expected to do even better when it was released later in the fall of 1915.

At this point Universal was offered a feature that had been filmed by a new company called Alco Films. The company was unable to arrange distribution and offered the completed film to Laemmle. It was *The Garden of Lies,* starring Jane Cowl (who was in the later hits, *Lilac Time* and *Smiling Through*). It was written by Justus Miles Forman, who died on the *Titanic.*

Once he made this plunge, Laemmle decided to go all the way. He organized Broadway Universal Features in imitation of Famous Players. In a trade announcement, he said:

> On July 12, under this new brand, Broadway Universal Features The Universal Film Manufacturing Company will release the beautiful star JANE COWL in *The Garden of Lies* in five reels.
>
> It was done for you, Mr. Exhibitor. The Universal was willing to sign the stars. It was willing to buy Broadway plays. It was willing to give them to you on the Regular Universal program. All it asks is that you do your part. That you get out and advertise these wonderful films. Advertise not only Jane Cowl, but all these wonderful stars: Emmett Corrigan, Marie Cahill, Marie Tempest, Julia Dean, Harry Vokes, Cyril Scott, Henrietta Crossman, Helen Ware, Lawrence D'Orsay, Hap Ward, Wilton Lackaye, Frank Keenan, Charles Evans, Blanch Walsh, Nat C. Goodwin and Henry E. Dixey.

Jane Cowl played a woman who secretly marries the prince of a mythical country. They have a car wreck on their wedding day. Before the girl regains consciousness, the prince is called home in a crisis. The girl, awakening, falls into a lassitude upon learning her husband has apparently deserted her. Her doctor, alarmed at her condition, gets Mallory (William Russell) to impersonate her hus-

Broadway stars, with the exception of Geraldine Farrar, had not been successful on the screen, but producers kept trying. In 1915 Laemmle formed Broadway Universal Features Company to star actors and actresses from the stage. Jane Cowl in *The Garden of Lies* was one of them.

band. At this point the girl is so disturbed in her mind that she can remember nothing except that she had been married and her husband refused to see her in her illness.

Mallory protests that it is impossible for him to impersonate her husband. The doctor assures him that it is possible and that it is the only way to restore her will to live. He claims that when she comes out of her trance and shock, she will not be able to remember Mallory or what happened during her illness.

Mallory agrees, meeting her in a beautiful garden that he mentally names the garden of lies, because

of the subterfuge. He grows to love her and she responds by improving.

At this point her prince husband returns. Seeing them together in the "garden of lies," he is infuriated. He challenges Mallory to a duel in which he is disarmed by the American. The princess is then shocked out of her condition. Realizing she has been tricked, she is infuriated. Then the vengeful prime minister, who has opposed the marriage, has her kidnapped because the king has just died and the prince is now king. It is unthinkable for him to be married to a commoner. In an attempt to rescue her, her husband is killed and she is reunited with the man who posed as her husband in "the garden of lies."

The story, which had great charm to both stagegoers and movie audiences of a bygone day, was one of Jane Cowl's great hits. It was surpassed only by her performance as the little French girl in *Lilac Time,* a role Colleen Moore played on the silent screen.

Jane Cowl came from New England and as a teenager became locally noted for "expression," which years ago meant recitations. This gave her stage ambitions. She was fortunate enough to interest David Belasco. He started her in small parts and gradually worked with her over several years. Finally becoming impatient with the deliberate way Belasco was building her career, she left the "bishop of Broadway," as Belasco was called, to take part in a play called *The Bamblers.* She scored a tremendous hit and then went on to play the lead in *Within the Law,* another hit that Norma Talmadge played on the screen.

After *The Garden of Lies,* Broadway Universal Features made a number of other films, including *The Earl of Pawtucket* with Laurence D'Orsay, the comedian. Unfortunately stars like Cowl, Julia Dean, and other Broadway luminaries did not shine as brightly on the small-town screens that Universal catered to as did purely movie-bred actors such as Grace Cunard and Francis Ford.

Also, there was exhibitor resentment of the higher prices asked for the Broadway Universal Features. Laemmle expressed surprise at the failure of theaters to book at the raised prices. He complained that he was only asking a slight amount more than he did for a regular five-reel program. Unfortunately this slight amount, added to the lack of drawing power of the Broadway stars, doomed Broadway Features.

Broadway Universal Features followed the Zukor formula of Famous Players in Famous Plays. This one features the comedy star Lawrance D'Orsay in his stage hit, *The Earl of Pawtucket.*

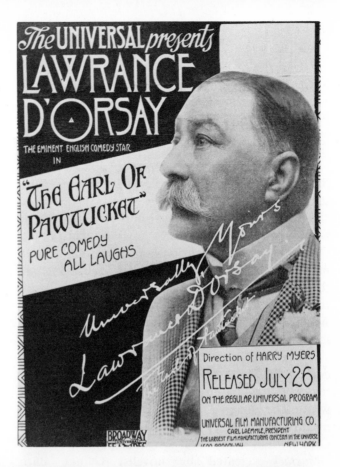

The 1915 serial, *The Broken Coin,* again pitted Grace Cunard against Francis Ford. Harry Mann is with them in this still.

Lasky and Zukor did better because they had more big-city outlets where audiences were more sophisticated. Universal catered more to small-town and rural audiences. These preferred the action movies for which Big U was famous. And they continued to get them.

Among the top money makers of 1915 was *The Broken Coin,* perhaps the best of the Ford-Cunard serials.

Episode one was released June 21, 1915. Kitty Gray, a San Francisco newspaper woman (Grace Cunard) finds in a curio shop a half of a coin inscribed with a cryptic message: "Underneath flagstone of north corner torture cham be found treasures valuable s the Kingd Gretzhoffen Mi." After she leaves, an agitated foreigner arrives looking for the coin.

Kitty realizes that the message on the broken coin is the key to a treasure. For some unknown reason that the author, Emerson Hough (who also wrote *The Covered Wagon*), did not reveal, Kitty decides that the other half of the coin is in Gretzhoffen, a mythical kingdom patterned after *Graustark,* created by novelist George Barr McCutcheon.

She gets permission from her editor to go. The editor was played by Carl Laemmle. Laemmle told Grace that he knew she had hoped to reduce the budget by getting him to play the cameo role for nothing, but that she was wrong. He insisted on being paid five dollars, which he received by check. At the end of the film he was required to play a return engagement in the final reel. He spent over two-hundred dollars for train fare and hotel bills to make the return and again collected his five dollars salary.

On the boat the foreigner who tried to find the coin follows and tries unsuccessfully to steal it from Kitty. Suspecting that she is to be robbed, Kitty fools the thief by putting a handkerchief and an American half-dollar in a bag.

Arriving in Gretzhoffen, she finds the king is a puppet dominated by sinister Count Frederick (Francis Ford). The king has the other half of the coin. The rest of the film revolves around the struggles of Count Frederick to get both halves of the broken coin.

Eddie Polo, a former circus acrobat, played the sinister foreigner who first trailed Grace Cunard. Later, after he was severely beaten by Prince Frederick for failing to get the broken coin from Kitty, he begins to aid the girl in her struggle.

Jack Holt was also in the cast.

Not all Universal films depended upon violent action, however. Laemmle especially loved sentimental tearjerkers and constantly urged his production people to find more stories like that. Such suggestions were pretty much the extent of his interference with actual production. He was a businessman and engrossed in the business side, especially advertising, which was controlled by Bob Cochrane. He did try to see every film made by Big U and could be very caustic about pictures he believed were below the Universal standard. Once at IMP, before Big U was formed, he withheld forty-five films, worth about forty-five-thousand dollars because he felt they were substandard.

The kind of picture he is said to have liked is *A Bit O' Heaven,* which Eclair released in 1915. It was a one-reel, featuring child actress Clara Horton and Eve Mansfield.

Faith (Clara), about ten years old, sells papers to keep her and her younger sister (Eve) from starving. Their father is dead and their mother is a brutal drunkard.

The mother dies and Faith takes Eve with her to sell papers. A charity worker hears of their plight and tells them that if they are good little girls God will take care of them. The charity worker then leaves, promising to do something for them later.

The two little girls go back to selling papers. In the meantime, in the house of rich Mr. Marbury (Lindsey Hall) a birthday party is being arranged for his ten-year-old motherless daughter. But she runs into the street and is killed.

This is not known to Faith and Eva, who keep wandering about the streets looking for God, whom the charity worker told them about. Growing tired as evening comes, they sit down on the stoop of a brownstone front mansion and fall asleep. Faith is so hungry that she dreams that she is seated at a table and God is serving her wonderful things to eat.

Inside the house Marbury, grieving for his lost child, looks at the loaded table set for the party she would never have. Unable to bear the sight, he puts on his coat and starts to leave the house. He sees the sleeping children. He awakens them and is struck by how much Faith is like his own lost child. He takes them inside to the loaded table.

Faith is overcome. She thinks her dream has come true and that Marbury is God, serving her wonderful food. Marbury hears their story and calls his housekeeper to prepare the girls a room. They will stay with him forever.

Stuart Paton, who was moving into the front ranks of Big U directors, decided one day in 1915 that Jess Willard would make a great actor. Jack that Paton was certain that Willard would be a great drawing card. Julius Stern, Eastern operations manager, okayed the idea and Paton sold Tom Jones and Jack Curley, Willard's fight managers, on the idea. Paton claimed that the wide advertising would help the fight gate.

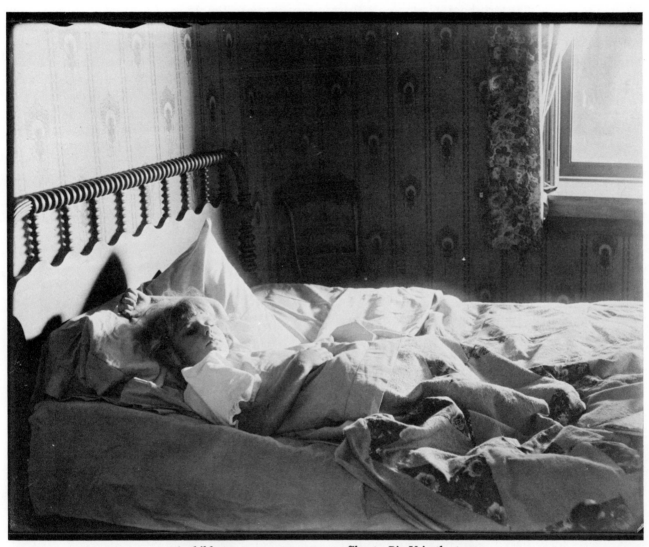

A child star was as necessary as film to Big U in the teens. Clara Horton made several pictures, including *A Bit O' Heaven* in 1915.

Johnson was then heavyweight champion prize-fighter of the world. And throughout the racist country there was frantic searching for a "white hope" to take the Black Johnson's crown. They thought they had it in tough Jess Willard from Arkansas. The coming bout raised such interest

The idea almost collapsed when the managers asked one-thousand dollars for the services of their "white hope." Some frantic talk with Stern and finally a presentation of the idea to Laemmle himself overcame this block. Willard was promised the thousand. Unfortunately negotiations had gone on so long that Willard was scheduled to leave for his training camp. He could spare only one day for the film.

It was only set to be a one-reeler, but even so one day was but one-third of the time Paton usually put in on a one-thousand-foot film.

He had gone too far to back out, he figured. He told the managers to have their man at the studio at daybreak. They'd start shooting as soon as there was light. Nothing doing! Their boy was in training for the fight of the century. He had to have his full sleep quota. They would be there at eight in the morning and it would be necessary to quit at five.

"Then *be* there!" Paton said.

He had written the script himself. It was called *The Heart Punch.* It was the story of the fighter whose wife objected to him being in the ring and how their tiny daughter brought them together again. Katharine Lee was the child. Marie Wierman was the woman. Tom Jones and Jack Curley played reallife roles as Willard's handlers. Comics Bobby Vernon and Bert Roach had roles, as did Howard Crampton and Allan Holubar.

Paton started off with the gym scenes. They went off easily with Allan Holubar sparring with Willard. The Fairmont Athletic Club in New York had been rented for the sequence. And two-hundred *supers* were hired to make up the audience. Apparently the word *extra* hadn't come into vogue at this time, for a publicity release on this film referred to *supers,* a stage term. Lights were provided by banks of mercury vapor lights crews had installed the previous night.

After the fight scenes were finished, Paton rushed his crew and actors across to the studio at 111 E. 14th Street for the interiors. Because of the short time, he had arranged all the sets and rehearsed everybody, including three-year-old Katharine Lee, so there would be no delay.

As the clock ticked merrily toward quitting time, troubles started. Katharine Lee, who had been rehearsed with Allan Holubar taking the Willard role, couldn't understand the change and kept yelling for her old friend to come back. Then Willard, who had come through beautifully at the gym, got embarrassed trying to play the love scenes with Marie Wierman. The frantic director chased all but the essential people off the set. This didn't help at all. There was still a director, cameraman and electricians around.

Muttering an order to keep the camera going,

Paton said, "We'll shoot to the last minute and then pick the least worst of the shots."

Despite his misgivings, the reel turned out well enough. Paton told Laemmle and Stern that everything had gone smoothly, but privately he confided to friends that he'd never use a real prizefighter again as long as he lived.

Frank Lloyd was another later famous name to contribute to the flood of pictures that poured out of the "Largest Film Manufacturing Concern in the Universe." Lloyd later made such famous films as *A Tale of Two Cities* (Fox) with Dustin Farnum, *Oliver Twist* (First National) with Lon Chaney and Jackie Coogan, *The Sea Hawk* (First National) with Milton Sills, and won an Academy Award for *Cavalcade,* in 1932.

Frank Lloyd, who years later won an Academy Award for direction, began his career as an actor for Universal. Here he is in *His Last Serenade,* made in 1915.

At Big U he doubled as both actor and director. *His Last Serenade,* made in 1915, is an example of his work. It was released under the Laemmle brand, a new addition to the list of releasing companies.

Lloyd played Beppo, an old Italian street violinist, who used to enjoy playing special tunes for Helen (Helen Leslie) the small daughter of Millard K. Wilson and Gretchen Lederer. The girl had always been crippled. Now her health has taken a turn for the worst.

When the doctor leaves the house, shaking his head sadly, Beppo asks how his little friend is doing. "She hasn't a chance to live," the doctor says. "She seems to be missing something. I wish I knew what it is."

Heartbroken, Beppo moves up to the window where he hopes Helen can hear and begins to play the gay little tunes she loves so much. Inside the house Helen hears the music. Her face brightens. Her overjoyed parents call the doctor back and Helen asks for Beppo. They bring in the old musician to play for her. She falls asleep and the doctor tells them that she will recover. Beppo smiles, but does not tell them that as his friend is recovering, he will be dying himself and that this was his last serenade.

In mid-1915 the director list at Big U stood at Francis Ford, the Lois Weber and Phillips Smalley team, Otis Turner, Henry McRae, Murdock MacQuarrie, Robert Z. Leonard, Frank Lloyd, Charles Giblyn, Robert Daley, Allen Curtis, Clarence Badger, Al Christie, Horace Davey, Sidney Ayres, Joseph de Grasse, and Lon Cheney (sic) who was directing J. Warren Kerrigan and Vera Sisson. One of the pictures listed for the incorrectly spelled Chaney was *The Service of the Sword,* based on a George Bronson short story of the same name. This feature film, which is not listed in the usual Chaney filmographies, supposedly had Chaney in a small supporting role.

According to *The Movie Magazine* of June 15, 1915, Francis Ford was considered the top Universal director at this time. Editor Wycliffe A. Hill said of Ford: "Mr. Ford is known to all his friends, relations and colleagues as one of the best-natured men in the world. He apparently is entirely devoid of captiousness, ill-humor or nervousness. It can be truthfully said of him that he is the most gentlemanly of all the world's great producers."

Casting at Universal, before things became more businesslike, was somewhat casual. A passing face, a friend visiting the set, or an odd happening that caught a director's eye — all these as well as direct applications — often led to successful movie careers. Vera Sisson, before she married and left the screen, was one of those who became a movie star due to a chance visit to a set. This was not unusual. The Gish sisters got their start because they dropped in to see Mary Pickford one day at Biograph.

In *For Cash,* 1915, Lon Chaney played Vera Sisson's father in addition to directing.

Vera Sisson lived with a widowed mother in Central City, Colorado, a mining town in the mountains above Denver. She had never acted or had any desire to do so. In 1913 she and her mother came to California, with little Vera laboriously lugging a heavy box of ore samples given to her over the years by Central City miners. She was very proud of the samples and always took her visitors in to see them in later years.

She heard that a cousin, Edith Bostwick, was playing in pictures and went to Edendale where the Victor Company had been squeezed in with IMP and a half dozen others. Joe MacDonald (later famous as J. Farrell MacDonald) was directing the Victor Company in a picture with Edwin August and Jeanie Macpherson (who became Cecil B. DeMille's script writer). Edith Bostwick was playing the other woman.

Edith called MacDonald's attention to how pretty Vera looked. He, lacking any other opportunity, cast her as a maid.

"All I had to do was come in a couple of times and dust some chairs," she recalled later. "But I was very nervous. I must have run up to Edith a hundred times to keep asking her if my makeup looked alright."

When MacDonald left to go with a new company called Venus Features that intended to release through the Mutual organization, he took Vera with him. Venus did not pan out and she worked for Reliance. She then came back to Universal to work in Joker comedies before Jacques Jaccard selected her for the J. Warren Kerrigan company. After Jaccard dropped out temporarily following a quarrel with H. O. Davis, studio manager, Lon Chaney took over the company for a series of six pictures in 1915. Chaney neither liked directing nor was he very good at it. He went back to full-time acting and screen immortality.

A typical juvenile male lead of the 1915 period was Raymond Gallagher. His career followed the well-worn groove. As a child in San Francisco he became enamored of the stage. Although his father insisted he go to college and study electrical engineering so he could support himself in later years, young Ray only had eyes for the stage.

He celebrated his graduation by packing his degree in his trunk and applying to a local stage manager for a job. He got a walk-on role in *Resurrection,* the Russian tearjerker, and went on to play juvenile leads in stock for five years. He then landed a supporting role with David Belasco in *The Girl of the Golden West.*

When this famous old melodrama closed Gallagher met Gaston Melies, who was in New York to organize a French branch of his brother's famous Parisian operations. He was also frantically trying to find ways to keep American producers from duping the fantastic films that Georges Melies was making.

Melies took Gallagher on a round-the-world filming tour. He left the company in Japan to work for Lubin. Lubin had seen Gallagher in a Melies film that Lubin had stolen and duped for sale. He spent only a year with Lubin, for Universal — in keeping with a company policy — offered him more money and better billing to switch to them.

In the strictly comedy field Eddie Lyons topped all the others in popularity. He often teamed with Lee Moran in a continuation of the *Hallroom Boys* films that Moran had made with Neely Edwards. In the beginning Lyons was often teamed with Victoria Forde, the daughter of an old time character actress, Eugenie Forde. Vicky Forde made a multitude of pictures with Lyons and the Lyons-Moran combination.

Vicky in those days was cute as well as pretty and — as someone characterized her — a bundle of laughter with skin stretched over it. But at the close of each day's work neither the cast nor the director ever expected to see her again in the morning. The reason was that she was met each evening by a young man from Selig who arrived in a sports roadster that he drove like he rode his horses in his Selig films — that is to say, one notch above breakneck speed. All predictions that he would kill himself in a car finally came true, but not until the 1940s when he failed to see a road detour.

But in between these years, Tom Mix became a legend and the husband of pretty Vicky Forde. After Tom carried her off to Selig as his costar, Lyons and Moran worked with a succession of pretty girls, several of whom went on to greater glory.

The most famous graduate of the Lyons-Moran films was Betty Compson. Betty was born in 1897 and grew up in a succession of mining towns until her father died in 1912. She went to work at fifteen as a violinist in a theater orchestra. One day when an act failed to appear (bad liquor seems to have been the reason) Betty hastily devised a gypsy costume in imitation of a well-known variety star and put on a spirited gypsy dance while playing her fiddle.

This led her to join with a couple of young men in a touring act that got stranded. She and her mother then became housemaids until Betty could get another stage job. While touring, an actor friend gave her a letter of introduction to Al Christie, who was then directing comedies for Universal's Nestor company.

She contacted Christie, who offered her forty dollars a week. *Motion Picture News,* in its issue of

November 6, 1915, reported: "In honor of Miss Compson's arrival the Nestor Company began filming an appropriate subject: *Wanted, A Leading Lady.* Her first picture dealt with the trials of a movie director trying to shoot a college life picture. The complications revolved around the antics of Lee Moran and Eddie Lyons to gain Betty's favor."

In 1915 Laemmle released *Jeanne Dore* with Sarah Bernhardt and "Little Jacques." With them is Louis Mercanton, the director of the French film. Bernhardt played all her scenes sitting because she had just lost a leg in an operation and couldn't yet stand on her artificial one.

As for Lyons himself, Eddie started as a member of a newsboy's singing quartet that took him into vaudeville. He finally ended up on Broadway in the play *Mrs. Wiggs of the Cabbage Patch.* He next appeared in *Beverly of Graustark.* When this ended and nothing else opened up for him, he was glad to accept Al Christie's offer to join Lee Moran in comedy films. The team lasted for over six years.

In 1915 Universal scored a real scoop in obtaining U.S. distribution rights to *Jeanne Dore,* which Louis Mercanton had made in France with Sarah Bernhardt. Movie historians make much over Adolph Zukor's presentation of the "Divine Sarah" in *Queen Elizabeth* but are strangely quiet about Laemmle's exhibition of *Jeanne Dore,* a much better picture than the amateurish earlier film. It was the story of a mother forced to watch the execution of her beloved son.

The play, by Tristan Bernard, was a stage vehicle for Miss Bernhardt when she was forced to undergo an operation that removed her leg. *Motion Picture World* said, "Owing to her inability to walk with her artificial leg, all the scenes show her either sitting or standing. Madame Bernhardt appears in over a hundred scenes in this production. She took the greatest possible interest in the details of the scenes. This enthusiasm is reflected in her work. Never, it is asserted, has she acted more magnificently." Another writer said she did not look a day over forty. She was then seventy.

Other stars of 1915 included Wallace Reid and his wife, Dorothy Davenport, who started with Big U in 1914. They played in a number of pictures. Reid's best picture in 1915 was *The Test,* in which he worked with Frank Lloyd. Robert Z. Leonard and Ella Hall continued their team with a genuine hit in *Mavis of the Glen,* the story of a young bride who is snubbed until it is discovered that she is a famous actress in disguise.

Hobart Bosworth was another pioneer who made the trek to Big U this year. Bosworth, a stage actor, had settled in Southern California after catching consumption. When Francis Boggs of the Selig Polyscope Company arrived in 1909 to make the first film in Los Angeles, he asked Bosworth to join his company. After some hesitation, Bosworth agreed. He stayed with Selig until 1914, when he helped form Bosworth Productions, which was partially financed by Oliver Morosco for release through Paramount. Bosworth left the company in 1915 after a quarrel over policy. Phillips Smalley and Lois Weber, who had left Universal to join Bosworth, returned to Big U at this time and suggested to H. O. Davis that he sign Bosworth.

In addition to pictures with other units, Bosworth was put into one of the Broadway Universal Features. He hardly qualified as a Broadway star himself, but the picture, *Colorado,* by Augustus John, had been a Broadway hit, thus

The shy maiden Robert Z. Leonard finds on an island turns out to be a disillusioned actress who had fled from her theatrical world in the 1915 film *Mavis of the Glen,* with Ella Hall as Mavis.

Frank Lloyd, right, proves to Wallace Reid that he has the making of a man by subjecting him to *The Test,* a two-reeler released in 1915.

qualifying. The movie with Bosworth did better than most of these with genuine Broadwayites.

Colorado was in seven reels, an epic length for Big U. The publicity group told exhibitors that such a picture would cost them twenty-five to sixty-five dollars rental from producers like Lasky and Zukor. "But how can you make money at prices like that? As a Broadway Universal Feature it is released on the regular Universal Program at so slight an advance in cost over the regular seven-reel feature program that any Exhibitor can book it."

Some of the Universal pictures that closed out 1915 were:

The Measure of Leon Dubray, November 2, with Hobart Henley and directed by Henry Otto.

When Beauty Butts In, November 2, in which Vic Potel cavorts with bathing beauties in imitation of Sennett.

The White Feather Charge, November 4, with Rupert Julian and Elsie Jane Wilson. Probably suggested by *The Four Feathers* of A.E.W. Mason. It deals with the old custom of sending a white feather to one who is a coward. Julian also directed.

The Reward, November 5, with King Baggott and Edna Hunter. Directed by Universal's Director -General Henry McRae.

And as a sidelight on operatic history, Jack Cohn's Animated Weekly cameramen induced the great Enrico Caruso to join their ranks. The newsreel men went down to New York harbor to photograph the "King of Tenors" who was returning to Italy to sing *La Boheme.*

According to *Universal Weekly:* "Jack Cohn and Cameraman U. K. Whipple suggested to the youthful matinee idol that he take their camera and turn

The White Feather Charge, made by Rupert Julian in 1915, was praised for its realistic battlefield scenes.

it on the legion of cameraman who were photographing him."

Caruso happily agreed and Cohn, of course, shared with every still photographer and movie man shots of Caruso grinding the camera but Big U was the only newsreel company who could advertise that they had film shot by the great tenor himself.

Cohn was an exceedingly resourceful executive. He made the Universal Animated Weekly tops in the newsreel field during the years that he ran it. Later he left Universal to join his brother, Harry, in starting Columbia Pictures. While Harry Cohn, as chief of production for Columbia in Hollywood, got all the publicity, Jack Cohn in New York was the executive genius that complemented Harry's picture-making ability. Their partnership was remarkable considering that the two brothers reputedly hated each other.

7 Young Lon Chaney

Of all the hundreds of actors who cast their shadows on Universal screens in the nineteen years that Big U and its predecessor, IMP, made silent films, Lon Chaney achieved the greatest heights. Not only that, but Chaney made his two greatest films, *The Hunchback of Notre Dame* and *The Phantom of the Opera,* at Big U. *The Hunchback* is not only Chaney's best performance, but one of the greatest in the history of films.

A lot of misinformation has grown up around Chaney. Lon himself contributed to it. It is the nature of actors to dramatize and even to lie like hell to interviewers to make a story more interesting. Chaney was no exception. This is no more apparent than in a *Collier's* magazine interview given after the success of the *Phantom.* Some of the things he told Kyle Crichton in this article are absolutely at variance with the facts as shown by a careful study of stills of his makeup.

Chaney did not have any mysterious makeup secrets as some have insisted. He used standard stage and screen techniques. The exact bent wires that he used to uptilt his nose in the *Phantom* were described in a 1899 interview with May Robson, a quarter century before Chaney made *The Phantom.*

This is not to deride one who may well be the greatest screen actor of all time. It is to suggest that if one studies his makeup carefully, using clear stills instead of screen images, one will see that — surprisingly — his makeups were very simple in most cases. And this is the remarkable thing about them. The King of Makeup did not use nearly as much as his fans thought and still think.

This is true even of his *tour de force* makeup as the grandfather in *Mr. Wu* at MGM in 1927. The only makeup used in this tremendous presentation was to pull his eyes into a slant with glued fishskin and to draw wrinkles onto his face with a stick of grease paint liner. The wrinkles were staccato lines and not even blended. This shows clearly in original stills. The rest consisted simply of those enormous eyeglasses, a hood draped in folds to give the appearance of gauntness to his face, and pursed lips.

Similarly his excellent makeup as the Chinese in *Outside the Law,* Universal 1921, consisted only of slanting his eyes and inserting gutta percha teeth. The rest of this uncanny makeup consisted solely in *acting* like a Chinese.

Lon Chaney was born April 1, 1886 in Colorado Springs, Colorado. Both his parents were deaf and mute, but their four children were normal. In later years Chaney attributed his ability in pantomime to his attempts to communicate with his parents in sign language. In time he became a guide in the Colorado mountains, a carpet layer, and a paper hanger before drifting into show business with his brother, a stage manager in Denver.

Chaney was not the recluse in his early life that he was at the close of his career. He gave plenty of interviews — in fact, anytime he was asked. Close to the end — from about 1927 on — he decided it would enhance his mysterious image to withdraw.

In fact, in a 1929 interview with Harry T. Brundage, he said that he believed this to be good showmanship. In the interviews he did give, he was not always truthful, or at best told half-truths.

Outside the Law was a personal triumph for Lon Chaney as well as for the director, Tod Browning. A 1921 release.

In the Brundage interview Chaney said that he learned about acting and makeup from watching stars like Richard Mansfield whom he saw from the wings in the theaters where he worked.

This is very unlikely. John Chaney, who took Lon into the business, worked only in small theaters. Richard Mansfield played only the big houses. Also there is an enlightening article about Chaney in a 1916 *Universal Weekly* that throws considerable light on how he learned to make up for character roles.

He worked for some time in musical comedy. He couldn't sing, but was an exceptionally good dancer. He recited his songs, somewhat in the manner of Rex Harrison, according to his own statement. In the course of touring, he married, had a son, and remarried.

Then in 1912 the company he was touring with ended its run in Southern California. The manager decided to try for a foreign tour. Chaney decided against going along. One of the Chaney legends says he walked out to Universal and applied for a job. Since by his own statement, he was in Santa Ana, California, this would have been an unlikely walk of at least sixty miles.

In any event, he contacted Lee Moran, whom he had known in musical comedy. Moran got him an introduction to Henry McRae, who could always be depended upon to help a down-and-out actor. Chaney's face, which could be molded into any kind of role, got him steady work.

The first year of his work with Universal is a blank. His walk-ons and bit parts did not rate billing. In checking over old issues of *Universal Weekly* one occasionally sees faces that *might* be Chaney in old stills. One that definitely is him is the heavy-bearded burglar in the Phillips Smalley-Lois Weber picture, *Suspense,* released by Rex in early 1913 prior to Chaney's first billing in the Allan Curtis film comedy, *Poor Jake's Demise.* The Curtis comedy was released August 13, 1913.

Up to this time Chaney had played minor roles, foreigners, tramps, background characters, and the like. He had no real dramatic training. He had played only a few noncomic roles on the stage and these had been heavies. None had required heavy makeup. In an interview given around 1925 he stated that his first makeup role was in a picture he did not identify. But he did say it was a hunchback in a sympathetic role written by Jeanie Macpherson, who later gained fame as Cecil B. DeMille's script writer.

A review of Chaney's credits, such as are known, shows that the only picture recorded that fits this description is *The Sea Urchin.* The picture was written by Jeanie and directed by Robert Z. Leonard. Miss Macpherson, who had been trying to be an actress since she worked for D. W. Griffith, played the lead and Leonard played the hero. It was released under the Powers brand on August 22, 1913.

In the story, Chaney is a hunchback fisherman who loves Jeanie. He is enraged when she prefers Bob. The audience is led to believe that the hunchback intends to revenge himself on Bob, but when Jeanie is almost drowned, it is the hunchback who nearly dies to rescue her. In that ordeal he comes to realize that the girl's happiness means more to him than his own. Although she is ready to marry him out of gratitude, he gives her up to his rival.

This appears to be, from circumstantial evidence, the picture that launched Lon Chaney as a makeup artist. However, *Star of the Sea,* released January 10, 1915, is somewhat similar. The film, a two-reeler, was directed by Joseph de Grasse.

The cast included William Dowlan as the priest; Mr. Fenton as Mario, his nephew; Pauline Bush as Mary; Laura Oakley as Janice; and Lon Chaney as Tomasco, the fisherman.

The story is about Mario Busoni, a sculptor who aspires to be another Michelangelo. He is aided by his uncle, the priest, who secures a commission for the boy to carve a Madonna and Child for a cathedral in Naples. This is a great honor and will ensure the boy's reputation.

Mario has been carrying on with a jealous model named Janice, whom he leaves behind. In Naples Mario employs a young widow and her baby as models. Mary, according to the Universal prerelease announcement, is as beautiful "as sunset on the Bay of Naples."

Janice follows Mario to Naples and is enraged to learn that he has fallen in love with Mary and intends to marry her. She enlists the assistance of a hunchback fisherman named Tomasco, who had hoped to marry Mary himself. They plot to destroy Mario's statue. This will prevent him from achieving the reputation he seeks and will delay his marriage.

The night before the dedication they creep into the garden where the statue is sitting under drapes. Tomasco is transfixed by the beauty of the statue and is unable to swing his sledge. Janice takes it from him, intending to destroy it herself. As she does the statue opens its eyes and looks at her with such pained sorrow that Janice drops the sledge and falls to her knees. She and Tomasco began to weep.

At this moment the bishop and his priests file in. They mistake the two vandals for worshippers and file out silently.

The opening of the statue's eyes was not made with trick photography. Pauline Bush was clothed in a robe covered with plaster and her face and arms were covered with thick white grease paint and powder. She held a doll in her arms. She sat still until told to open her eyes.

In those days Chaney could play anything and do it convincingly. *Her Escape,* released December 27, 1914, had him cast as a blind gangster who tries to force his sister to steal from her husband. He was properly menacing, but his blindness was not too good since he played the role with his eyes open. Later as Pew in *Treasure Island,* he rolled his eyes up so that only the whites showed. In the *Road to Mandalay* he is said to have covered his eyeball with egg membrane. He had not learned these tricks when he made *Her Escape.*

The story involves Pauline (Pauline Bush) who becomes disgusted with her family's life of crime. She runs away. Her vindictive brother, Pete (Lon Chaney), follows her. She is rescued from him by a

Pauline Bush (Mrs. Allan Dwan) tries to break away from her revengeful blind brother, Lon Chaney, in the 1914 film *Her Escape.* Joseph de Grasse directed.

handsome miner, Paul (William Dowlan), who knocks Pete down.

Paul and Pauline fall in love and marry. In the meantime Pete has been blinded in a barroom brawl. Through a dope addict friend (Richard Rosson) he learns of Pauline's marriage to the rich miner. He gets Dopey to lead him to his sister's home. He threatens to kill her unless she agrees to steal money for Pete from her husband. Pauline breaks away and runs. Pete tries to follow, but blindly stumbles and kills himself falling down the stairs.

Chaney then did a completely change of pace as the cuckolded count in *Threads of Fate*. This film, like so many in which Chaney played the antagonist part, didn't make him out a true villain as he was in *Her Escape*.

The story was by Tom Forman, later a well-known actor, and directed by Joseph de Grasse. It was released by Rex as a two-reeler on February 21, 1915.

The Girl (played by Pauline Bush) goes to live with a rich aunt just as the Man (played by William Dowlan) grows tired of an empty life and becomes a wandering musician.

The Girl and the Man meet when she stops to listen to him play his violin. They are attracted to each other, but become separated. Despondent at the separation, the Girl agrees, at her aunt's wishes, to marry the Count (Lon Chaney). For this role Chaney wore chin whiskers, a monocle, a top hat, and a string tie.

It is an unhappy marriage. Then at a watering place she attends with the Count, the Girl again hears the Man's violin. The two meet secretly and, unable to live without each other, they agree to run away together.

The vengeful Count pursues them. At this point, the Man, with the Girl's agreement, turns their car over a cliff and the two unhappy lovers die together.

Threads of Fate opened and closed with a hand-colored allegorical scene of the Three Fates of mythology weaving life threads of humanity. In the closing sequence, the Three Fates pick up the broken strands symbolizing the Girl and the Man and tie them together. This was intended to signify that the lovers were reunited in death.

In a 1914 picture called *The Measure of a Man* Chaney got billing although his part was the minor one of Pauline Bush's father who opposes her marriage to a handsome gambler, William Dowlan.

In this picture Joseph de Grasse, the director, played the other man who gives up Pauline so she can return to her husband.

De Grasse also played a role in *Where the Forest Ends*, a two-reel Rex film released March 7, 1915. The story was an original written by De Grasse's wife, Ida May Park.

Rose (Pauline Bush) an uninhibited child of the forest, meets Paul Rouchelle, an artist, played by Lon Chaney. Paul persuades her to accompany him back to the city. She soon tires of the gay life and returns to the mountains where she plans to marry her old sweetheart, a ranger, named Jack Norton (William Dowlan). Paul comes to persuade her to go back with him. Jack learns for the first time of her sin. Paul flees when Jack tries to shoot him. When Jack spurns Rose because of her past, an old ranger, Silent Jordan (Joseph de Grasse), takes Jack to the grave of a woman Jordan similarly spurned, which he now deeply regrets. Stirred by Silent Jordan's sad tale, Jack forgives Rose and they are married.

The Desert Breed, directed by De Grasse from a Tom Forman scenario and released by Rex in March 28, 1915, was a change of pace for the entire Pauline Bush company. It was a genuine western. The story bears a faint resemblance to the Ford-Cunard film *Three Bad Men and a Girl*.

Jack (William Dowlan) and his sidekick, Fred (Lon Chaney), are chased out of Rawhide by the sheriff and his posse. On the edge of the desert they stop at the home of Jessie (Pauline Bush), where they ask for food. She lives alone and locks the door. Jack picks the lock, but she confronts them with a gun. Ashamed at the way they tried to force themselves upon her, they withdraw.

They are scarcely out of sight when three members of the sheriff's posse arrive at Jessie's place. Finding her alone, they try to force their attentions upon her. Hearing her cry out, Jack and Fred rush back and overpower the three men, handcuffing them to a post with their own cuffs.

They tell the girl that they are fugitives and she agrees to guide them across the desert. The sheriff arrives after they leave, but elects not to follow for he is certain they will die in the wasteland.

They almost do. The waterhole has dried up. Fred (Chaney) was shot in the earlier fight. He begins to rave and thinks Jack is one of the enemy. Jack is saved by Jessie's intervention. Then she finds water and they are saved.

She turns back home at the edge of the desert.

Joseph de Grasse, the director who did so much to help Lon Chaney get started, took the role of Silent Jordan in *Where the Forest Ends.* Here he keeps angry William Dowlan from shooting Chaney, an artist who seduced poor Pauline Bush, right. The film, a two-reeler under the Rex brand, was released in March 1915.

Jack and Fred look back and see her silhouetted against the sunset. She waves and they wave back. Iris out.

In *All for Peggy,* March 18, 1915, release, Chaney played Seth Baldwin, a middle-aged horse trainer, whose daughter, Pauline Bush, disguises herself as a boy to ride the winning horse in a race. She also wins a husband at the same time.

After several pictures in which he played semi-villains, Chaney was a double-dye rascal in *The Sin of Olga Brandt.* Olga, to get money for her invalid sister's care, sells herself to a wicked lawyer, Stephen Leslie (Lon Chaney). She later marries a young parson. There is a stir in the small town where they live over the showing of a motion picture called *Shall We Forgive Her?* The story of this film within a film parallels the sin of Olga Brandt.

Deacon Jellicoe (Charles Manly) leads a fight to have the film censored. The theater owner fights back in court, retaining Stephen Leslie as lawyer. Leslie recognizes Olga and threatens her with exposure if she does not return to him.

Her husband has gone to the theater to see a screening of the questioned picture. The committee has agreed to abide by the parson's decision. Olga writes her husband a letter confessing all that has happened and goes to the train station.

At the theater the parson praises the picture and upholds the moral of forgiveness that it preaches. "Judge not that ye be not judged," he said. He then goes home and is stunned to find his wife's letter of confession.

Leslie (Chaney) has also been affected by the picture. He sees Olga at the station and begs her to return to her husband, promising he will never threaten her again. The parson, at first confused and undecided what to do, remembers the picture and takes his wife in his arms.

This picture was said to have been suggested by Laemmle, who was then involved in censorship fights that threatened to remove some of his pictures from the screen.

Chaney's biggest break in 1915 was being cast in *Father and the Boys*, released December 2, 1915. The six-reel film, directed by Joseph de Grasse, qualified for Broadway Universal Features because it was from the Broadway hit written by George Ade. Digby Bell, from the original cast, was the star.

According to a story in *Moving Picture Weekly*, Bell became quite fond of Lon Chaney. The story claimed that Bell, learning of Chaney's interest in character roles, took the young actor to his dressing room and showed him more than two-hundred character makeups.

Bell's role in helping Lon Chaney become a master of makeup has not been mentioned since this original article appeared sixty years ago. It is probably true. Chaney was a minor member of the Universal stock company at that time. There was no particular point in publishing the story if it had not been true. Prior to this time Chaney had not used any elaborate makeup in any of his roles. In fact, he did not use a really elaborate makeup until he made *The Hunchback of Notre Dame*, in 1923.

However, old stills show that Chaney's character makeups improved after Bell's lessons in 1915. A story in a 1916 issue of *Moving Picture Weekly* harkened back to the work with Bell the previous year. It said that Chaney amused Bell during the making of *Father and the Boys* by making up to look like Bell.

The plot of *Father and the Boys* was a comedy of errors. Bessie, a Western orphan, owns a supposedly worthless mine. She comes to New York and is befriended by Bell, a rich man. Bell's sons, played by Harry Ham and Bud Chase, think their father is about to elope with a fortune hunter. In the ensuing mixup the boys fall in love

Australian Louise Carbasse had her name changed to Louise Welch for *Father and the Boys,* a 1915 release, but later it became Louise Lovely. In this scene she is with Lon Chaney.

with the girls father had picked for them. Bessie finds happiness with Tuck, an old sweetheart, who came to find her. Lon Chaney was Tuck and Louise Carbasse was Bessie.

Miss Carbasse came from Australia, where her parents had been associated with opera and the stage. She became quite well known in her own country. She came with her manager to the United States where she failed to set the world on fire and applied to Universal for work.

Father and the Boys was her first American picture and the name Carbasse was difficult to pronounce. It was changed to Welch, but Laemmle didn't like that. According to an article by Marjorie Howard in *Moving Picture Weekly:* "Mr. Laemmle, the Universal's president, came to the rescue. 'As she is so lovely, why not call her so?" he said. No sooner said than done; lovely she was and Lovely she became. So as Louise Lovely she starred at

Universal until the 1920s, when she went to Fox to finish her career. She was no newcomer to films when she joined Big U. She made ten in Australia.

The Grip of Jealousy, released February 28, 1916, gave both Miss Lovely and Chaney good, meaty parts. Chaney played Silas Lacey, a villainous planter in Southern plantation days.

Through a very involved plot a boy and a girl from feuding families secretly marry. A baby girl is born of the union just as the father is forced to flee to escape a false murder rap. The mother dies and the mother's sister (Louise Lovely) thinks the child is illegitimate and leaves her on the doorstop of an old slave named Jeff. Jeff has a pretty daughter who is molested by wicked Silas Lacey. This slave girl dies and Lacey, who owns Jeff, thinks the baby girl Jeff has is his own illegitimate daughter by the dead girl. Silas Lacey leaves the baby to be raised by Old Jeff. Virginia is the only one who knows that the child is really white and not born a slave.

Jay Belasco draws his gun to protect lovely Louise Lovely in Joseph de Grasse's *The Grip of Jealousy,* released in February, 1916 as a five-reel Bluebird feature.

The child, Linda, grows up to be a very lovely girl. She is coveted by Silas Lacey's son, not knowing that she is supposed to be his half-sister. Virginia, to protect the girl from becoming the mistress of young Lacey, agrees to marry Lacey senior if he will free Linda.

Young Lacey, outraged at losing the girl, kidnaps Linda, but she is rescued by her real father who has returned. Virginia reveals the girl's true identity. It is established that Lacey committed the murder Linda's father was accused of doing.

Chaney's makeup consisted of a black wig combed across his forehead. He also sported a handlebar mustache. The story was by Ida May Park and directed by her husband, Joseph de Grasse.

Chaney's next film was a society drama. He played a man whose wife had given birth to an illegitimate daughter before their marriage. She left the child with foster parent who died. She needs a new home for the child and confides in a family friend, Haywood Mack, whose wife, seeing them talking, becomes jealous. Complications develop, but all ends happily. *Moving Picture Weekly* said, "Chaney, in the principal part, has a role rather different from his usual style." His makeup was limited to light hair and a clipped, dark mustache. The picture, *Tangled Hearts,* directed by Joseph De Grasse and written by Ida May Park, was released April 2, 1916.

His next role was that of a Sicilian father seeking revenge. Giovanni (Chaney) had a beautiful wife (Louise Lovely) and a baby daughter. Leonita, the wife, is enticed aboard a yacht of the Betrayer (Haywood Mack). She leaps overboard, rather than sacrifice her honor, and is drowned. The Betrayer then returns to America. Giovanni follows, seeking revenge. The daughter, Elisa (again Louise Lovely), grows up. She is asked to dance at a rich man's party. Giovanni, suspicious, follows her and discovers that the host is the Betrayer. He kills the Betrayer and commits suicide by jumping out the window. The film, released as *The Gilded Spider,* on May 6, 1916, was directed by Joseph de Grasse from a story by his wife, Ida May Park.

Closing out 1916, Chaney played such diversified roles as the backstage *Bobbie of the Ballet,* the castaway who helped tattoo a treasure map on Louise Lovely's back in *The Grasp of Greed,* a doctor in *If My Country Should Call,* a crippled half-breed in *Place Beyond the Winds,* and a put-upon householder in *Felix on the Job.*

Lon Chaney, as Giovanni, is outraged to find his daughter, played by Louise Lovely, dancing at a party given by millionaire Haywood Mack (right) in the climax of *The Gilded Spider*, 1916.

Despite claims of some biographers that Chaney was poorly treated at Universal, the facts show otherwise. He worked constantly. He had full freedom in creating his own makeups and interpretation of roles. Both Ida May Park and Joseph de Grasse encouraged him. He was given, although only a supporting actor, a full feature article in Universal's trade magazine, *Moving Picture Weekly.* It was unusual for a supporting actor to receive this much space.

The Chaney story, published without copyright notice in the December 2, 1916, issue, was titled, "Making Up With Brains." The photographs mentioned in the story were printed on pulp paper and are too poor in quality to reproduce here. However, the picture of Chaney as Pancho Villa, the famous Mexican bandit chief, is remarkable.

The complete text of the article is as follows:

Lon Chaney, who appears in the Bluebird photoplay, *The Price of Silence,* has declared that, given time, and a well-filled makeup box, he will guarantee to change his countenance into that of any other person, and then will stand up to the test of being photographed for comparison with the original. If you will take a look at the two reproductions on this page, you will decide to agree that he can make good his boast.

76

It would be dangerous to bet against his declaration. The picture of the personage in the sombrero is not the latest portrait of Francisco Villa, but the result of several hours of work by Mr. Chaney on his own features. His attractive countenance is reproduced opposite this masterpiece of makeup, in order to show the magnitude of the task he undertook.

There have been many stories about his prowess in the art of disguise, especially the one of his turning himself into a reproduction of Digby Bell, while that veteran actor was playing in feature production at Universal City [*Father and the Boys,* 1915]. After studying these two cuts we can easily believe them.

Chaney makes no secret of the methods of his art, and is always willing to give the benefit of his experience to others. When asked how he manages to accomplish these extraordinary results, he gives the celebrated answer of Sir Joshua Reynolds when he was asked with what he mixed his paints — "With brains, sir."

Chaney is interested in faces as other men are interested in fine pictures or beautiful china. An unusual countenance gives him something of the pleasure that a collector experiences in a rare specimen of art which he collects. He studied the remarkable face of the bandit leader in reproductions that appeared in newspapers, and just as a tour de force, decided to imitate them. The result was so extraordinarily successful that he was persuaded to preserve it by photography.

Chaney appears in the forthcoming Bluebird photoplay *The Price of Silence* in the support of Dorothy Phillips. He has to portray a doctor, first in youth and then in middle age. He does this without the use of a white wig, whiskers, beard or overhanging eye-brows, yet there is easily 30 years difference between his looks in the first reel and in the last. He accomplishes this difficult effect "with brains."

Chaney used to be famous as an eccentric dancer, and has never lost his love for his art. Whenever there is a dance scene in a photoplay under production, he is pretty sure to be found an interested spectator. Dorothy Phillips realized this, and asked his advice and assistance in the new De Grasse picture in which she has to dance [*Hell Morgan's Girl*].

The aging effect in *The Price of Silence,* which the article writer commented on, was achieved by rubbing aluminum powder in the temples of his hair to achieve a silvery effect and by deepening the lines of his face with a grease pencil liner. More formal clothing in the final sequences heightened the effect.

Chaney's first release in 1917 (January 11) was the *Piper's Price.* The story was by Mrs. Wilson Woodrow, who, Universal liked to keep informing the public, was President Woodrow Wilson's cousin by marriage. Dorothy Phillips, who had worked her way up through the comedy ranks, was the star.

The film was a domestic triangle with Chaney in a sympathetic role. Ralph Hadley (William Stowell) marries Amy (Dorothy Phillips) after divorcing Jessica (Maud George). Jessica, an emancipated type, constantly has business contacts with her ex-husband. Amy thinks that there is more than business in these contacts. And indeed Ralph is considering divorcing Amy to remarry Jessica. Jessica is agreeable until she learns that Amy, unknown to Ralph, is pregnant. When Ralph comes to ask Jessica if she will remarry him after he is freed from Amy, Jessica introduces him to Billy Kilmartin (Lon Chaney), an old sweetheart, whom she has married that afternoon. She then tells Ralph that he will become a father and sends him back to Amy.

This was William Stowell's first Universal film. One reviewer said of it: "Mr. Stowell's good looks and sincere acting will win him many friends. Mr. Chaney needs no introduction. His work has already won him a sincere place. His role in *The Piper's Price* is something new for him, in that there is not a spark of villainy about it."

Lon Chaney as the blackmailing doctor in the 1917 film *The Price of Silence* **with Dorothy Phillips.**

In the next release, March 5, 1917, the same trio, Dorothy Phillips, William Stowell, and Lon Chaney, hit the jackpot with the biggest hit Universal had between *Traffic in Souls* in 1913 and *The Hunchback of Notre Dame* in 1923. This blockbuster was *Hell Morgan's Girl,* a milestone in the careers of both Dorothy Phillips and Lon Chaney.

Hell Morgan's Girl went into production as a programmer under the direction of Joseph de Grasse, working from an Ida May Park scenario based on a story by Harvey Gates.

Prior to the completion of the picture, the Universal marketing group began exploiting the picture for "State's Rights" sale. This meant that the picture was offered to independent exchanges within certain territory at a set price. Then the exchanges marketed the film for what they could get in their exclusive territory. The Big U propaganda hailed the picture as "the type of film that makes States Right buyers reap a golden flood of profits. A picture that is there with the punch that pulls the crowd — that packs them in at every performance. A tremendous dramatic production telling the most human story ever filmed. Lavishly produced; thrilling scenes of the great San Francisco earthquake; life in the famous Barbary Coast District of the city by the Golden Gate. Extra special paper [that is, advertising posters, lobby cards, etc.]. Choice territory still open. Communicate immediately with the State Rights Department of the Universal Film Mfg. Co., Carl Laemmle, President, 'The Largest Film Mfg. Co. in the Universe,' 1600 Broadway, New York."

However, when the film was screened in the Big U projection room in the Mecca Building in New York, Laemmle — who tried to see every Universal release — saw immediately that it was better than usual. He reminded his staff that the previous year the Big U special, *20,000 Leagues Under the Sea,* had similarly been a sleeper that made too much money for the States Right purchasers and consequently less for Universal. Laemmle thought they should withdraw *Hell Morgan's Girl* from its States Right offer and market it through the Universal subsidiary, Bluebird Photoplays, Inc. This was quietly done before States Rights buyers were aware of the quality of the film.

The publicity department then made an all-out drive, featuring huge cuts of Dorothy Phillips in her lowcut dancehall girl's dress with such tantalizing copy as:

> You may trust her
> You may hate her
> You may absolve her
> You may condemn her
> You may love her
> You may hate her
> But no matter how you feel toward her, you'll
> say she is WONDERFUL
> Come and see HELL MORGAN'S GIRL!

The story: Roger Curwell (William Stowell) is disowned by his rich father when the boy refuses to give up the life of an artist. Down and out, Roger wanders into Hell Morgan's saloon where he disparages a nude painting over the bar. Hell Morgan (Alfred Allen) has him beaten, but he is rescued by Morgan's daughter, Lola (Dorothy Phillips). Lola persuades her father to give Roger a job playing the piano. Roger paints Lola's portrait and they fall in love to the rage of Sleter Noble (Lon Chaney), who wants Lola himself.

Olga, a vamp who threw over Roger when his father disowned him, visits Hell Morgan's place on a slumming party. The father has just died, leaving his fortune to Roger, who does not know it. She makes a play for Roger and fiery Lola denounces them both. Roger leaves the saloon and Lola, brokenhearted, agrees to give herself (without marriage) to Sleter. She backs out when they get to her room. Noble tries to take her by force. Hell Morgan hears the noise and rushes in. Sleter shoots Morgan before he is overcome himself. Lola helps her wounded father down the fire escape to get away before Sleter recovers consciousness. When they reach the ground, the San Francisco earthquake occurs. Sleter is killed. Lola and Hell Morgan get to a refugee camp where Morgan dies and a remorseful Roger finds Lola.

Dorothy Phillips was perfect as the fiery Lola. Margaret MacDonald, critic for the *Moving Picture World,* took a lofty attitude about the film's moral character: "To the adult seeking for entertainment in reviewing the most vicious type of life, that which was common to San Francisco's Barbary Coast in the years gone by, *Hell Morgan's Girl* will exactly fill the bill. We could not recommend it, however, for refined audiences or for children. While it may be a perfect typification of that hole of vice, the realism of its staging makes it the more

responsible for high-priced but low-grade features that have weakened many exhibitors.

The BLUEBIRD announced its policy of "The Play's the Thing" in the most extensive moving picture advertising campaign ever launched, in the *Saturday Evening Post.* Every one said that BLUEBIRD was wrong.

Now — not only the fans and the Exhibitors and the Exchange men are convinced that BLUEBIRD was right, but OTHER PRODUCERS ARE ATTEMPTING TO FOLLOW THE BLUEBIRD LEAD.

What's the answer? BLUEBIRDS are getting the money. That's all there is to it. If you want to pack your house; add prestige; and popularity to your theater's reputation; increase your bankroll; and QUIT WORRYING ABOUT YOUR SHOW — BOOK BLUEBIRD photoplays.

Despite Laemmle's claims, pictures without stars did not draw at the box office — not for Universal nor for any other movie producer. Once the star system got underway there was no return to the cradle days of films when actors were anonymous.

The curious thing is that at no time were Bluebird films starless. In fact, Laemmle siphoned off the cream of Big U's films and casts for Bluebird releases. An example is the pulling of *Hell Morgan's Girl* off the States Rights circuit for Bluebird release.

The first Bluebird release had Helen Ware, a famous Broadway star, in the leading role. *The Grasp of Greed,* based on an H. Rider Haggard novel, had Louise Lovely's name above the title in the star's position. This ad, typical of those for Bluebird, was more artistic and restrained than most of Universal's ads. It was printed in red, blue, and black inks. Curiously, it billed Lon Chaney, a supporting actor, above Jay Belasco, who played the hero.

Other top stars who appeared in "starless" Bluebirds were Lois Weber and Phillips Smalley in *Hop — the Devil's Brew;* Carter de Haven in *The Wrong Door;* Hobart Bosworth and Yona Landowska in *The Yaqui;* J. Warren Kerrigan in *The Gay Lord Waring;* Florence Lawrence in *Elusive Isobel;* Harry Carey in Edward LeSaint's *Three Godfathers;* Tyrone Power in *The Eye of God;* and others with Rupert Julian, Lois Wilson, Mary Fuller, Ella Hall, and Herbert Rawlinson. Later they added Mae Murray. And you can bet that they billed the temperamental Miss Murray as a star. In fact for her second Bluebird, Mae's name was in letters twice the height of the title.

Mae joined Universal in 1917. In 1916 the cast roster was listed in an ad which claimed:

NO PROGRAM ON EARTH can even begin to show anywhere near such a list of screen stars as the list below shows. No program on earth gives you the stories, action or sets as the tremendously successful Universal Program. Week after week you get the cream of the world's biggest Box Office attractions on the mighty Universal Program

Mildred Adams	George Hernandez
Stella Adams	Lee Hill
King Baggott	H. L. Hicks
Harry Benham	Allan Holubar
Mother Benson	Jack Holt
Curtis Benton	Little Clara Horton
Henry Bergman	Alice Howell
Clara Beyers	John R. Hope
Hobart Bosworth	Billy Human
Paul Bourgeois	Mina Jeffries (Cunard)
Neal Burns	Rupert Julian
Harry E. Carey	Thomas Jefferson
Harry Carter	J. Warren Kerrigan
Lon Chaney	Yona Landowska
Fred Church	Florence Lawrence
Wallace Clark	Pathe Lehrman
Harry Coleman	Robert Leonard
Betty Compson	Gretchen Lederer
Peggy Coudray	Louise Lovely
Howard Crampton	Ethel Lynne
Doc Crane	Eddie Lyons
Juan de la Cruz	Cleo Madison
Charles Conklin	Edna Maison
Grace Cunard	Charles Manley
Dorothy Davenport	Luella Maxim
Carter De Haven	Violet Mersereau
Flora Parker De Haven	Matt Moore
Harry Depp	Lee Moran
Eugene Derue	M. Moranti
Charles W. Dorian	Harry Morris
William C. Dowlan	W. F. Musgrave
Frank Elliott	Harry Myers
Marjorie Ellison	Eva Nelson
Adele Farrington	Frank Newberg
Marc Fenton	Jane Novak
Francis Ford	Eva Novak
William Franey	Laura Oakley
Mary Fuller	Charles Ogle
Thelma Francis	Louise Orth
Jane Gail	Paul Panzer
Ray Gallagher	Val Paul
William Garwood	Peggy Pearce
Douglas Gerrard	Carmen Phillips
Maud George	Dorothy Phillips
Joseph W. Girard	Eddie Polo
Olive Fuller Golden	Victor Potel
Myrtle Gonzales	William Quinn
Ray Griffith	Herbert Rawlinson
Ella Hall	Stella Razeto
Gilmore Hammond	Ned Reardon
Harry R. Haskin	Billie Rhodes
Hobart Henley	Billie Ritchie
Gale Henry	Franklin Ritchie

BLUEBIRD
Photoplays (Inc) Present
LOUISE LOVELY
in THE GRASP
OF GREED
With Lon Chaney & Jay Belasco
Adapted for the Screen from
"Mr. Meeson's Will" by Sir. H.
Ryder Haggard. Directed
by Joseph DeGrasse.

Bluebird Photoplays was organized by Laemmle to market
the company's quality films and the Bluebird advertising
was handled with greater taste than the average Universal
exploitation. In this ad for *The Grasp of Greed*, originally
printed in two colors and black, Jay Belesco tattoes a map
of a gold mine on Louise Lovely's back. Lon Chaney assists.

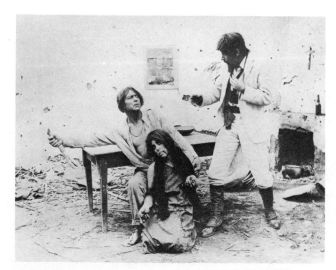

Hobart Bosworth and Yona Landowska with Alfred Allen in *The Yaqui,* a 1916 Bluebird release.

Mark Robbins	Lule Warrenton
Edith Roberts	Lois Weber
Rex de Rosselli	Glen White
Jack Scharrer	Ben Wilson
Gertrude Shelby	Elsie Jane Wilson
Ernest Shields	Lois Wilson
Master Antrim Short	William Worthington
Phillips Smalley	William Welch
Frank Smith	
Richard Stanton	
Richard Sterling	
Rosemary Theby	
Agnes Vernon	
Fatty Voss	
Marie Walcamp	
H.M. Wallack	

Of the women on this list the two who went the

Rupert Julian was Scrooge and William Worthington the ghost in *Marley's Ghost,* Universal's attempt to improve on Charles Dickens's original title, *A Christmas Carol.*

farthest were Betty Compson, who achieved stardom with her role in Paramount's *The Miracle Man,* and Lois Wilson, who also went to Paramount.

Lois Wilson trained to be a school teacher, but a friend submitted her picture to a beauty contest. She won and came to Hollywood, where she became leading lady for the J. Warren Kerrigan company. After leaving Universal, Paramount's teaming her again with Kerrigan in the historic *The Covered Wagon* made her a star.

The two most important pictures of 1916 were *The Bugler of Algiers* and *20,000 Leagues Under*

J. Warren Kerrigan stands off a full saloon of toughs in the 1916 film *The Measure of a Man.* A film by the same name was released by Universal in 1915. Its cast included Chaney, Dowlan, and Bush.

the Sea. The *Bugler* was Rupert Julian's second greatest hit as an actor. His greatest was in *The Kaiser, the Beast of Berlin.* He was a good, versatile actor, but his chief fame lies in his work as a director. He completed *Merry-Go-Round* after Irving Thalberg fired Erich Von Stroheim from the film, and did all but the final chase sequence for Chaney's *Phantom of the Opera.* This alone secures his cinematic fame.

Julian was the son of a New Zealand sheep rancher. His parents sent him to college to train for the Catholic priesthood. He repaid their solicitude by running away to serve in the Boer War. He was captured, escaped, and made his way to the coast where he caught a tramp steamer and got back to

83

Naked Hearts, 1916, was based upon the poem *Maud* by Tennyson. In the foreground are Zoe Beck and Antrim Short. The film was directed by Rupert Julian and released by Bluebird.

Louise Carbasse Welch Lovely prevents Rupert Julian from killing Douglas Gerrard in the 1916 Bluebird film, *Bettina Loves a Soldier.*

Rupert Julian treats Zoe Beck for rattlesnake bites in the 1916 one-reeler *The Desperado*. Jack Holt played the sheriff pursuing Julian.

The Blackmailer, played by director Rupert Julian, is foiled by the cleverness of Elsie Jane Wilson in a 1916 short written by Raphael Sabatini, author of *Captain Blood*.

South Africa. He rejoined the army and received a battlefield commission as second lieutenant.

After the war he drifted into acting. In the United States he received an introduction to Lois Weber and Phillips Smalley, who gave him his basic screen training. He began as an actor, but advanced to actor-director, playing the lead in most of his films. Some of his successes prior to *The Bugler of Algiers* were *Naked Hearts,* based on Tennyson's poem *Maud, The Evil Women Do* with Francilla Billington and Elsie Jane Wilson, *Bettina Loves a Soldier* with Doug Gerrard and Louise Lovely, *The Desperado* with Zoe Beck and Jack Holt, and *The Blackmailer* with Elsie Jane Wilson.

In *The Desperado* Julian is a vicious badman fleeing from the sheriff, played by Jack Holt. The title identified Julian as "the worst cuss in the hull state of Oklahomy." In his flight he comes across a covered wagon driven by a man with his wife and small daughter. The daughter (Zoe Beck) wanders

The Bugler of Algiers was Rupert Julian's biggest hit as an actor, even eclipsing his performance as *The Kaiser, The Beast of Berlin,* in 1918. In this scene he is shown with Ella Hall and Kingsley Benedict.

off and is bitten in the leg by a rattlesnake. She is found by Julian who uses his gun barrel to tighten a tournaquet about her leg and sucks the poison from the snake bite with his mouth. This caused his own death. When Sheriff Holt catches up with him, he has a change of heart about Julian's character and letters a slab for the desperado's grave: "God aint agoin to be too hard on a man who gave his life for a little kid." The picture irised out with little Zoe clutching a homemade doll Julian had made for her and praying for the soul of the bad man who gave his life for her.

Julian was very well received in this role. One critic said it was his best since *The Dumb Girl of Portici,* in which he supported the famous dancer Anna Pavlova the previous year.

The Blackmailer was directed by Julian from a short story by the famous Rafael Sabatini, author of *Captain Blood* and *The Sea Hawk.* The Blackmailer threatens the Woman with letters of hers he has in his possession. She tells him to return the next day and she'll have the money. He returns and is admitted by a housemaid he has never seen before. The maid removes her wig and discloses the Woman. She tells the Blackmailer that she dressed in a maid's disguise and rented a room, establishing her identity as another woman. Now she intends to shoot him. Then she will leave the house as the maid and vanish. Later she will return as the Woman and discover that her new maid murdered the Blackmailer. When she pulls a small revolver, the frightened Blackmailer gives her the letters and flees.

The plot of *The Bugler of Algiers* was more involved. It was taken from a book by Robert H. Davis and Perley Poore Sheehan.

Anatole, played by Kingsley Benedict, enlists as a bugler to fight with the French in Algiers in the 1840s. He is joined by his friend, Pierre (Rupert Julian). In Algiers Anatole is captured by the Arabs. He is ordered to sound the retreat on his bugle, but at the risk of his life courageously sounds "Charge." The French advance and win the battle. Pierre is able to rescue Anatole.

Years pass before they can return home. They find that Gabrielle (Ella Hall), Anatole's sister whom Pierre loves, has disappeared. They then set off for Paris where Pierre is to be decorated for his heroism in the Algiers war. On the way Anatole dies. Pierre passes himself off as Anatole and receives the medal. He finds Gabrielle in Paris.

Alan Holubar directed and starred as Captain Nemo in the 1916 version of Jules Verne's *20,000 Leagues Under the Sea.*

Together they go back to the village where Pierre places the medal on his friend's grave.

Other 1916 releases included *The Thread of Life* with Frances Nelson and Ben Wilson, *A Stranger from Somewhere* with Franklyn Farnum (no relation to Dustin and William), *Honor Thy Country* with Neva Gerber, *The Devil's Bondwoman* with Dorothy Davenport, and a curious Chaney item called *The Accusing Evidence.* The latter is listed as a "Special Big U Drama," and is a one-reeler released as a part of the regular program of Thursday, November 23, with Lon Chaney, Pauline Bush, and Murdock MacQuarrie. The two other films on the program were *The Emerald Pin* with Roberta Wilson, and *Irma in Wonderland,* a comedy.

The plot outline reads only: "Lon is a member of the Northwest Mounted Police and is in love with a little girl of the woods. He is accused of a breach of duty. Rather than have the morale of the corps suffer he submits to false evidence. Later he

The Williamson submarine doubled as the *Nautilus* in the
1916 epic *20,000 Leagues Under the Sea*.

is vindicated and the picture ends happily." The program lists the cast as Lon Chaney, Pauline Bush, and Murdock MacQuarrie.

This picture is not listed in the standard Chaney filmographies. Furthermore, Pauline Bush was no longer working with Universal when this picture was released. It might have been a reissue of an older picture, but ordinarily Universal labeled such pictures as reissues. In any event, the plot does not coincide with the listed Mounted Police films Chaney made with Bush: *Bloodhounds of the North* and *The Honor of the Mounted* in 1913. It is possible that it is an old picture that had not been released earlier for some reason.

The big picture of 1916 was *20,000 Leagues Under the Sea* with Allan Holubar as both star and

director. The picture was based upon the Jules Verne novel of an Indian rajah who loses his beloved wife and daughter. He then builds a submarine and has tremendous undersea adventures. Holubar played Captain Nemo.

The punch of this picture was the extraordinary underwater photography scenes by the Williamson Brothers. Previously underwater films were shot in tanks, but these scenes were made in the Atlantic Ocean near the Bahamas to take advantage of clear water, the coral formations, and the colorful fish.

The photography was made possible by two inventions. One was a collapsible submarine tube invented by Capt. Charles Williamson. It was made of steel plates covered with rubberized cloth to keep the water out. Williamson's sons, Ernest and

George, mated their father's tube with a round steel ball set with a thick window in the side, through which the cameraman could photograph. It resembled the later bathysphere used for deep sea exploration. The brothers also developed a submarine light. They enclosed a Cooper Hewitt mercury vapor lamp (developing twenty-five-hundred candlepower) in a waterproof casing. Then eight such lights, developing twenty-thousand candlepower, were lowered into the sea in front of the photographer's chamber. Insulated wires carried current from generators on the barge to which the collapsible tube was attached. The high candlepower was necessary because of the slow film then in use.

The picture was a huge success, but because of the high cost of the underwater scenes the picture did not make a great deal of money. This strengthened Carl Laemmle's opinion that features were ruining the industry.

Last of the Ford-Cunard serials was the 1917 film *The Purple Mask,* about a society girl who lead a Parisian apache gang for kicks.

Universal continued to push serials. Grace Cunard and Francis Ford made *Peg O' the Ring,* a fifteen-chapter film that opened May 1, 1916. The original announcement said this would star Ruth Stonehouse and Eddie Polo, although the scenario had been prepared by Grace Cunard for herself and Francis Ford. They were taken off the film for undisclosed reasons and the Stonehouse-Polo announcement was made. Grace made a quick trip to New York to see Carl Laemmle personally. Big U then announced that the film would star Ford and Cunard. An inquisitive viewer wrote the Answer Man at one of the fan magazines asking what had happened. He was told, "It was just a family affair and no one else's business." It was, however, the next to last serial for the Ford-Cunard team. The next serial after *Peg* was *Liberty, Daughter of the USA,* with Marie Walcamp and Jack Holt. Then on December 31, 1916, Universal released the last of the Ford-Cunard serials: *The Purple Mask.*

The Purple Mask was a melodramatic mishmash

Grace Cunard is threatened by the terrible dangers she brought on herself as both star and script writer for *Peg O' the Ring,* the 1916 Cunard-Ford serial.

The nude women in this scene from *Dante's Inferno* did not wear flesh colored tights. An examination of the original print (which came from Grace Cunard's personal collection) shows that the nipples of the woman in the right foreground had been retouched out to give the impression of tights. And in three of the women in the back the breasts were reduced in size by the retoucher.

that recalled the earlier *My Lady Raffles* series that they had made. Grace is a lady Robin Hood and Francis Ford is the detective pursuing her.

Pat Montez dearly loves a joke. So when her rich aunt puts her jewels in a wall safe, Pat "steals" them. This brings in Detective Phil Kelly, who wears a top hat and a stripe-lined cape. In the ensuing chase Pat (Grace Cunard) becomes leader of a group of apaches in Paris.

The scene then shifts to a mythical kingdom and then to New York. Pat continues to play the crook. In one episode Pat steals a necklace from the bride of a man and then sells the necklace back to the bridegroom for ten-thousand dollars, which

Pat gives to the girl the man left with a child when he deserted the mother to marry another girl.

According to the announcement of the picture: "In America Pat helps unfortunates by stealing from the rich, turning the proceeds over to the unfortunates, keeping a small part as her 'commission.' After each crime she always left a purple mask as her trademark so that no other might be blamed for it."

Finally deciding that she loves the detective, Pat forsakes her Robin Hood life and becomes Mrs. Phil Kelly.

The year 1917 was not a good financial year for Universal, despite the successful pictures that were made. The entrance of the United States into the European war caused prices to rise, squeezing Big U's profits. Then a number of male actors rushed off to join the army, causing other disruptions. The higher cost of the five-reel features of Bluebird and Red Feather further drained the treasury. Laemmle asked his actors to take a cut in salary. Betty Compson, who was making comedies with Lyons and Moran, said later she was asked to take a fifty percent cut.

The pictures, however, continued to roll out of the film factory. One notable one was a Ford-Cunard version of *Dante's Inferno* with a half-nude Grace Cunard guiding Francis Ford (in top hat and lined cape that he wore in *The Purple Mask*) through Inferno. The odd attire was nothing unusual for Ford. He played Sherlock Holmes in the 1914 two-reeler, *A Study in Scarlet,* wearing a big cap instead of the traditional Holmesian fore-and-aft deer stalker.

Another 1917 picture was *Pay Me!* This was Universal's attempt to repeat the success of *Hell Morgan's Girl* with the same cast, Chaney, Stowell, and Dorothy Phillips. Allan Holubar made a fantasy called *Sirens of the Sea.* It had Jack Mulhall, Carmel Myers in her first lead, Louise Lovely, and baby Ben Alexander. Franklyn Farnum starred in *The Scarlet Car,* a ridiculous story by Richard Harding Davis. In this film Lon Chaney played a madman who thought he was a descendant of Paul Revere. He had papers that would clear up a mystery, but thought he could give them to no one but Revere. So Farnum dressed as Revere and rode up shouting, "Give me the papers! I'm Paul Revere!"

Roy Stewart, an old Griffith alumnus, joined Universal, making *The Fugitive* with Louise Lovely. Mack Swain left Sennett to join L-KO, bringing his Ambrose character. Swain, a great comedian, is best remembered as the sourdough who thought Charlie Chaplin was a chicken in the starving scene in *The Gold Rush.*

The Universal Jewel trademark was introduced in 1917. Jewel was invented to cover films that Laemmle thought were better than usual. The Chaney-Phillips film *Pay Me!, The Man Without a Country, Sirens of the Sea,* and Lois Weber's *Price of a Good Time* were early Jewel releases.

Serial releases for 1917 included the last fifteen chapters of the sixteen-chapter *The Purple Mask, The Gray Ghost* with Harry Carter and Priscilla Dean, *The Mystery Ship* with Ben Wilson and Neva Gerber, *The Red Ace* with Marie Walcamp, and *The Voice on the Wire* with Wilson and Gerber.

Rupert Julian and Ruby Lafayette in the sentimental 1917 Bluebird production *Mother O' Mine.*

The big name to push out of the ranks in 1917 was Harry Carey, Universal's answer to Selig's Tom Mix and Ince's William S. Hart.

Unlike Mix and Hart, who had western roots, Harry Carey was a New Yorker. He was the son of a judge and was sent to law school to prepare himself for a legal career. Instead, amateur dramatics led him to the stage. After getting his seasoning with the Yorkville Stock Company and the Rand Opera Company (which did not put on operas), he joined a "Tom" company. First he played Simon Legree and then inherited the Uncle Tom role. Of this role he said, "Uncle Tom is a fat role for an actor. It is like they say of Kentucky whiskey, it can't be bad."

He then wrote a western melodrama called

Monroe Salisbury and Ruth Clifford in *The Door Between,*
a story of the trials of young married life, directed by
Rupert Julian and released in 1917.

Montana. When no producer would touch it, Carey
borrowed money from his father and staged it
himself.

"We played it for eight years," Carey recalled
once. "I made a bundle of money out of it. So I
wrote another play, *Two Women and That Man.*
Three weeks later the show closed and I was flat
broke. That forced me into the movies and I
became a member of the original Biograph Stock
Company." He joined Biograph in 1909.

Here Carey worked with Mary Pickford, the
Gishes, Mabel Normand, Mack Sennett, Henry B.
Walthal, Lionel Barrymore, and Arthur Johnson.
He stayed with Biograph until D. W. Griffith left.
Then after a year and a half at loose ends, he
joined Universal in mid-1915. For all his Eastern

birth, Carey looked like a westerner and insisted on
what he called "barbed wire" type stories. His
stock boomed with fans and by 1917 he was the
cowboy king of Universal.

In motion picture histories Carey's name is
always associated with that of the great director
John Ford. Actually Fred Kelsey and Jacque
Jaccard made more Carey films than Ford.

A typical Carey film of the period was *The Bad
Man of Cheyenne,* a two-reel Bison directed by
Kelsey from a story by Carey. It casts the star in
his familiar role of Cheyenne Harry, a good-bad
man.

The sheriff's wife (Priscilla Dean) accidentally
scares a team of horses who run away with her
small daughter (Betty Janes.) The child is rescued

by Carey, the bad man from Cheyenne. Later in a saloon, an old man is shot. Before he dies he gives his collie dog to Cheyenne Harry. Harry has a fight with a gang of roughs over the murder of the old man. He is wounded and must hide out in the hills. The collie comes into town and steals food for Harry to keep him alive while he recovers. The gang tips off the sheriff that Harry is the wanted man from Cheyenne. Harry is captured and brought to town to be lynched. As the rope is placed around Harry's neck the sheriff's wife informs him that Harry saved their daughter's life. The sheriff (William Gettinger) draws his gun and shoots the hangman's rope in two.

According to publicity put out at the time, Carey wanted the hanging scene to look real. Ordinarily in hanging a man, the noose is arranged so that the victim's neck is broken as he falls through the gibbet trap. Carey arranged so that the box under his feet was removed slowly. Slowing the cranking of the camera speeded up the action so it appeared normal. Then he was suspended with the rope around his neck and his feet above the ground.

Pressure of the rope around his neck was actually choking, but a sharpshooter out of camera range was supposed to shoot the rope in two. He missed on the first shot and Harry choked longer

In an attempt to repeat the success of *Hell Morgan's Girl* De Grasse made *Pay Me!* with, from left, Claire DuBrey, Dick LaReno, Lon Chaney, Dorothy Phillips, Evelyn Selbie, and William Stowell.

93

The cast of *Sirens of the Sea* in 1917 line up for a photograph with their director, Allan Holubar (with megaphone and cigar). Jack Mulhall is at left. Carmel Myers (in her first lead) stands next to Holubar. Fourth cherub from the left (wearing shoes) is Ben Alexander. Louise Lovely is also in the lineup.

Lon Chaney plays a madman who thought he was the descendent of Paul Revere in the 1917 five-reel *The Scarlet Car*, which starred Franklyn Farnum. Directed by Joseph de Grasse.

94

Universal directors knew how to save set money. In the 1917 serial, *The Gray Ghost,* written by Arthur Somers Roche, director Stuart Paton borrowed Brock and Company's Los Angeles jewelry store to film a holdup scene in chapter 2.

the local audience would know the actors. The Ford family name was O'Fearna, which was anglicized to O'Feeney and finally to just plain Feeney.

After four years of working with his brother, Jack Ford starred in and directed *The Tornado* for 101-Bison, released March 3, 1917. In the story Lesparre (Duke Worne) robs a bank and kidnaps the banker's daughter (Elsie Thornton). Jack Dayton (Jack Ford) goes after them unarmed and brings the villains to justice. Ford also wrote the story.

Ford's first film with Harry Carey was released August 2, 1917. It was *The Soul Herder* for 101-Bison in three reels. A minister (Jean Hersholt) is slain and Cheyenne Harry (Harry Carey) takes his place to reform a town.

than he expected. The second shot severed the rope and Harry had to suspend shooting the film for the rest of the day to have his throat treated.

This sounds like one of Paul Gulick's publicity inventions, but those who knew Harry said he was capable of doing such a stunt.

But despite his other directors, Harry Carey is best associated with John Ford. Ford, then known as Jack, was Francis Ford's brother. As related earlier in this book, young Ford came to Hollywood to join Francis in 1913. He acted as prop boy, bit actor, and finally supporting actor for Francis and Grace Cunard. He graduated to playing leads in a few western shorts.

When Jack's pictures showed in Portland, Maine, his home town, the exhibitor painted out the Ford name on the posters and put either Jack Feeney or Frank Feeney, depending on whose film it was, so

Cheyenne Harry, the character created by Harry Carey, was Universal's king of cowboys until the rise of Hoot Gibson. A number of director John Ford's early films starred Carey.

9 The End of the Decade

The stars of the early teens were getting old and losing favor. New ones — former supporting actors for the old stars — began to take over the star roles for themselves. This was due partly to a growing sophistication among audiences. Francis Ford and Grace Cunard, for example, were "scenery chewers" and "emoters." The same was true of King Baggott. Newer actors were showing increasing restraint and more naturalism. Chaney, for example, was spending long hours in old clothes going through sections of Los Angeles observing characters in order to pick up real mannerisms.

Francis Ford left Universal. His 1918 serial *The Silent Mystery* was made for Burston. Rosemary Theby, a popular Universal leading lady in 1915 and 1916, was in the film, as was Mae Gaston, another who had deserted the Laemmle lots. Lois Wilson went to First National and then to Paramount. Wallace Reid also moved to Paramount. Frank Lloyd had given up acting and was forging ahead as a director at First National. Mary Fuller had gone and so had Ethel Grandin.

Lon Chaney was still around but he was preparing to move. After his big success in *Hell Morgan's Girl* in 1917, he thought he deserved more important roles. Instead he remained a stock actor who was shoved into any role where he was needed. This was exactly what he had been doing before.

Chaney's first release after *Hell Morgan's Girl* was *The Mask of Love,* a dreary role in which he played Mario, an underworld character who tries to attack the daughter of a man who has befriended

him. The role of Krogstad in Ibsen's *A Doll's House* and Joe Lawson in *Pay Me!* were the only meaty roles he had.

In the 1918 release *The Kaiser, The Beast of Berlin,* his role of Admiral Tirpitz (and everybody else's) was overshadowed by Rupert Julian's triumph as the Kaiser. Julian was so good that for years he was called in every time a director needed to show the Kaiser. After this film, Chaney stagnated in roles such as the girl's uncle in *The Grand Passion,* the newspaper editor in the Mae Murray film *Danger — Go Slow* (released December 9, 1918), and as a playboy in *The Talk of the Town.*

So after finishing *That Devil Bateese,* he left Universal to free-lance. Because of the backlog, several of his film were released months after he left. Chaney's first job away from Universal was with William S. Hart in *Riddle Gawne,* and the second was with Henry B. Walthall in *False Faces,* a Lone Wolf story by Louis Joseph Vance. Gretchen Lederer, whom he had directed at Universal, was also in the Hart picture.

Meanwhile back at Universal he had not been forgotten. Tod Browning, who had directed Chaney and Priscilla Dean in *The Wicked Darling* (released February 3, 1919), had not forgotten him. After making *A Man's Country* for Robertson-Cole (a role no better than he had been getting at Universal), Chaney returned at Allan Holubar's request to make *Paid in Advance* with Dorothy Phillips and Priscilla Dean. Browning

Rupert Julian did such a marvelous job impersonating the German ruler in *The Kaiser, the Beast of Berlin*, released in 1918, that for the next decade he was called in everytime it was necessary to show the kaiser. Here he is with Ruth Clifford, and Lon Chaney, who appears over Julian's shoulder. A seven-reel picture directed by Julian.

stopped Chaney on the lot and asked him to play the gangster role in a film the director was setting up. Chaney agreed, but a few days later came back to beg Browning to release him.

"George Loane Tucker has offered me the part of Frog in *The Miracle Man,*' he told Browning. "I talked to him about it before I said yes to you, but Tucker said then that he wanted a contortionist for the part. I showed him the way I'd play it and he said that he'd think it over. I thought I was out."

Browning had seen the stage version of *The Miracle Man,* staged by George M. Cohan. He knew

the Frog role was a natural for Chaney. He released Chaney from his obligation, but said, "The next time you won't get away so easily. I've got an idea that I haven't had time to work out, but there'll be two parts for you and they'll be good ones."

"Just let me know," Chaney replied.

It was two years before Browning got his idea in shape, but it proved to be the blockbuster *Outside the Law.*

Tod Browning was just developing his enormous talent in those days. He had been a racing jockey in Kentucky until he grew too big. He then joined a

Chaney again has a gangster role in the 1919 Tod Browning
film, *The Wicked Darling,* starring Priscilla Dean.

stock company and eventually played comedy roles for Triangle before shifting to directing at Universal. He had spent considerable time with circuses and carnivals in his youth and kept egging his Universal bosses to let him make films against these backgrounds. They refused. He had shown a talent for crook films and they kept him on these.

One of his major jobs was to build the career of Priscilla Dean, whose star was rising as that of Dorothy Phillips faded. Priscilla was destined to be Universal's major woman star in the first years of the 1920s. Her forte was playing wicked women who reformed in the last feet of the final reel. She was an exceptionally good actress and the public loved her.

Priscilla was born in the theater, debuting November 25, 1896, as the daughter of a well-known actress of the day, May Preston Dean. Her first stage role was at four in *Rip Van Winkle. Who's Who in Filmland,* published in England, said her film debut was at the age of twelve, which would be 1908. She does not mention this in any of her interviews.

She claimed she debuted in comedy leads for an unnamed quickie company. "The company was running on a shoestring," she told interviewer Truman B. Handy. "Some high official eventually absconded with the cash investment — in fact, with all the cash, salaries and everything."

Flat broke, she sent her mother a wire collect for money to pay her hotel bill. In the meantime she hitchhiked to Universal City, for someone had

98

told her Universal was a sucker for a sad story from stranded actors and actresses. They put her to work with Eddie Lyons and Lee Moran, but somehow or another she offended somebody — she never knew what the trouble was. She was called into the office and told that her forty dollars a week salary stopped as of that moment.

"Then I'll sit right here until it starts again!" she snapped.

She had the reputation of being quite a tempestuous person in those days. She was quite capable of sitting there screaming until she got work. So her forty dollars a week salary was restored after a ten minute break and she was sent over to join the company of an actor who took an instant dislike to her. He wanted no part of anyone with such a bombastic personality. He had her fired again. Priscilla, while she told this story in an interview, did not identify the actor except by the initial F. It certainly wasn't Francis Ford, since he had the reputation of being nice to everyone (with the possible exception of Eddie Polo, who was twice fired from a Ford picture for displaying an exaggerated ego).

Priscilla then knocked around the lot with first one group and then another until Joseph de Grasse put her in *The Wildcat of Paris,* the story of a spitfire character that just suited her. Priscilla's star then began to rise and after she teamed with Tod Browning in a series of crook dramas, headed for the upper rung of the ladder.

The year 1918 was also notable for the arrival at Universal of one of the most notable names in movie history — although he was hardly notable at this time. He was an Italian dancer whom Carmel Myers decided should be in her next picture. She kept bothering Paul Powell, the director, until he gave in just to shut Carmel up. Although the man had appeared in bit parts in three previous pictures, Carmel's *A Society Sensation* was his first billing. He was billed as Rudolphe de Valentina. Later he refined this into plain Rudolph Valentino.

Valentino had immigrated from Italy and appeared as a dancer in New York. Then getting work in a touring company, he got stranded in San Francisco and was brought to Hollywood by Norman Kerry who had known him in the East. He danced with Carmel Myers at a party Kerry got him invited to. Carmel thought he was great and set out to make him a movie actor.

Carmel herself was one of those who got into

Rudolph Valentino received his first screen billing with Universal. Carmel Myers, second from left, talked director Paul Powell into giving Rudy a part in *A Society Sensation* in 1918.

films in an improbable manner. She was a rabbi's daughter. It happened that her father helped D. W. Griffith on biblical research for *Intolerance.* The rabbi then suggested that perhaps his little Carmel would look very pretty in the movies. Griffith paid off his debt by giving her a bit part in the film and then promptly forgot her. Carmel was both pretty and determined and got herself some small parts at Universal by playing on her experience with Griffith. Then after Allan Holubar chose her for the lead in *The Sirens of the Sea* she began to climb.

Carmel Myers also insisted on Valentino for her next film, *All Night,* produced in 1918 by Paul Powell.

Valentino did well enough in *A Society Sensation* for Paul Powell to use him in Carmel's next picture, *All Night,* which was also released in 1918.

Then Mae Murray, who had known Rudy in New York, insisted that he be given a part in her Universal picture, *The Delicious Little Devil.*

Of all the shadows that ever moved across the silver screen, Mae Murray comes closest to being what the public envisions when they think of the words "silent movie star." She was even more the archetype than Gloria Swanson, which took some doing.

Mae wasn't really Mae She was Marie Koenig, but in later life she'd be damned if she'd admit that she was ever anybody but Mae Murray. As a child she fell in love with the dancing of Irene Castle and emulated her heroine so well that at fifteen she was in the chorus of Ziegfeld's Follies. Ziegfeld saw her in an Irving Berlin musical. Berlin in turn found her dancing in a nightclub.

She danced her way out of the chorus and was doing a specialty number called Mary Pickens, which was a burlesque of Mary Pickford, when Adolph Zukor brought her to Hollywood in 1916 to appear in the Mary Johnston historical film *To Have and to Hold.* Robert Z. Leonard, who had left Universal to direct for Paramount, directed her in several films. Then they were married (after Leonard got her out of a hasty marriage to Jay O'Brien) and went as a team to Universal. The Murray-Leonard team made eleven films before moving on. The films were *Princess Virtue, Face Value, The Bride's Awakening, Her Body in Bond, Danger — Go Slow, Modern Love, The Scarlet Shadow, What Am I Bid? Girl for Sale, Delicious Little Devil,* and the *Big Little Person.*

Valentino played in both *Delicious Little Devil* and *Big Little Person.* Both were released in 1919. Then after getting into one film each at Artcraft, Equity, Fidelity, Republic, Metro, and First National, Valentino came back to Universal City for his final picture under the Big U. banner. This was Allan Holubar's *Once to Every Woman,* with Dorothy Phillips.

It must be admitted that Valentino showed little promise in his Universal films. There is paradox in the story that Rex Ingram, the moody Irishman who first aroused interest in Valentino in the historic *Four Horseman of the Apocalypse* at Metro, refused to use Rudy at Universal in his 1920 film, *Under Crimson Skies.* This film, greatly

MAE MURRAY IN THE BIG LITTLE PERSON

The future Sheik, Rudolph Valentino, had a villainous role in the 1919 Bluebird Production of *The Big Little Person,* starring Mae Murray and directed by Robert Z. Leonard.

praised for its artistic photography, starred Elmo Lincoln, the "Mighty Man of Valor" in Griffith's *Intolerance.* Elmo is celebrated in movie history as the screen's first Tarzan (in *Tarzan of the Apes,* 1918).

The success of *Tarzan of the Apes* at National got Elmo a Big U bid and he appeared in the 1919 serial, *Elmo, the Mighty.* Grace Cunard, now fallen from favor, played the feminine lead, but her name was in small letters under the title. She never again regained her former position. In all, Elmo Lincoln spent four years at Universal.

With the fading of Grace Cunard, the big woman serial star at Universal was Marie Walcamp. After appearing in a long series of one- and two-reelers, Marie made her serial debut in 1916 with *Liberty, Daughter of the USA.* In 1917 she made *The Red Ace* in sixteen chapters and in 1918 filmed *The Lion's Claw* with Thomas Lingham. Lingham came to Universal from Kalem where he had been with Helen Holmes in *The Railroad Raiders.* When Kalem was sold Lingham, Helen Holmes and J.P. McGowan, Helen's husband and director, came to Universal. Helen and McGowan did not stay long.

Helen Gibson, ex-rodeo rider, replaced Miss Holmes at Kalem, but then she and her husband, whom everybody called Hoot, soon left to join Universal also. Miss Gibson left Big U in 1919, but Hoot remained to become the big western star of the twenties.

Marie Walcamp, the reigning serial queen in 1919, was born in Denison, Ohio, in 1894. She was in musical comedy for several years. She was with Kolb and Dill when Laura Oakley suggested that she try the movies. Laura introduced her to Henry McRae and she started, as so many girls did, with Lyons and Moran.

Marie made a variety of comedy and western two-reelers. Then in 1916 Jacques Jaccard, who had directed her at Universal, gave her a supporting role in *Patria*, the Irene Castle serial he was making for William Randolph Hearst. The picture's blatant war propaganda caused a controversy that got the film held up until 1917. Marie made a hit in her role, which led to her Universal serial starring roles.

Unlike many actresses who were contemptuous of serials, Marie professed to love them. In an interview in *Motion Picture Classic* she said: "I believe the serial is the savior of the motion picture industry. It's a sure bet. The serials are making money everywhere . . . Of course with me it's always the same old thing, I get chased, abused, nearly killed, rescued in the nick of time, hated — and finally there's a happy forever! The stories are very much alike in that respect, but the pleasure to the actress is in the many new locations."

In another interview, Marie commented on doing her own stunts. Carl Laemmle had very early established the rule that no actor or actress would be force to take any risk thought too dangerous.

"But what can you do?" Marie asked. "The director says, 'Now Marie, you don't have to do

Rudolph Valentino's last Universal picture was *Once to Every Woman* with Dorothy Phillips. Valentino played a man who was violently jealous of an opera star (1920).

CARL LAEMMLE presents

UNDER CRIMSON SKIES

A Glorious Romance of Love and High-Seas Adventure

TRULY, a great picture. A rousing, stirring picture. A romantic picture. A story that sweeps you up out of your humdrum life and carries you off to sea—to fight with strong, silent Elmo Lincoln against the perils of mutiny on the high seas—to fall in love with a beautiful woman and sacrifice liberty for her sake—to make a miraculous escape from the fetid dungeon of a southern republic and become master of a colony of beach-combers, conquering them by might of fist and brain and then—to save the one woman from a terrible fate in the midst of red revolution. Splendidly acted by a great company in outdoor scenes of tempest and sunshine rarely equalled for their marvelous photography.

Starring
ELMO LINCOLN

One of the few big productions of the year.

Directed by REX INGRAM *Story by* J.G. HAWKS

UNIVERSAL-JEWEL SUPER-PRODUCTION

Elmo Lincoln was with Universal for four years. Critics did not have a lot of enthusiasm for his acting in 1920's *Under Crimson Skies* but they were lavish in praise of the photography, which was due primarily to the artistic eye of director Rex Ingram, who stressed beauty in all his films.

The Universal backlot in the 1920s looked like a shanty town.

this if you don't want to. We'll get a double.' Everybody is standing there looking at you. How can you say no?"

The most popular male serial star was Eddie Polo. Polo was born in Los Angeles, California, in 1881. He claimed to trace his ancestry back to Marco Polo, the Venetian traveler to China in the thirteenth century. He came from a circus family and made his own debut as a baby clown at the age of four. Later he became a circus strongman. While

Marie Walcamp escapes from the roof of a burning house by swinging on a rope from a windmill in chapter 9, *The Human Pendulum*, of the 1918 serial *The Lion's Claw*. Thomas Lingham is set to catch her. Harry Harvey directed this chapter.

recuperating from injuries, he applied for work at Universal. Ford and Cunard used him in a number of shorts and in the serial *The Broken Coin*. This relationship ended when it became apparent that Polo thought he knew more than they did about making pictures.

After leaving the Ford-Cunard group Polo

HELEN GIBSON
IN
"THE ROBBER"

Helen Gibson, Hoot's first wife, succeeded Helen Holmes at Kalem and then moved to Universal for three years.

played with Marie Walcamp in *Liberty*, and in 1918 debuted as the star of his own serial, *Bull's Eye*. Bulls Eye was the name of a ranch and the story pitted sheepherders and cattlemen against each other. James Horne directed.

Bull's Eye was released February 9. Then on November 18, 1918, another Polo serial was released. It was *Lure of the Circus*, directed by J. P. McGowan. Josie and Eileen Sedgwick were in the cast. The Sedgwick sisters, in company with their brother, Edward Sedgwick, came to Holly-

Marked Men, with Harry Carey and Winifred Westover, 1919, was the best film made by director John Ford during his Universal period.

wood from Galveston, Texas. The girl, both athletic types, appeared in numerous westerns, while Ed, after a short spell as a comedy heavy, became a top director for Universal.

Polo then made *King of the Circus* and *The Vanishing Dagger* in 1920; *Do or Die* and *The Secret Four* in 1921. He left after this final serial to make his own pictures and failed.

The old-timers, Rupert Julian and Harry Carey, carried full schedules through 1918 and 1919. Jack Ford made one of his favorite silents with Carey in 1919. This was *Marked Men,* a remake of the Peter B. Kyne novel *Three Godfathers,* which Edward J. LeSaint made for Universal in 1916.

The story told about three bank robbers, played by Carey, J. Farrell McDonald, and Tom Gribbon, who find a dying woman with a child in the Mojave Desert. They decide that saving the child is more important than their own freedom. This was a repeat for Carey. He played the same role in the LeSaint version. Twenty-nine years after the 1919 film, Ford remade the story in 1948 and dedicated the film to the memory of Harry Carey. Winifred Westover, who later married William S. Hart for three months, was also in the picture.

This was also the year that two of Hollywood's legendary people made their debut at Universal. They are Erich Von Stroheim and Irving Thalberg.

Von Stroheim, like Mae Murray and Gloria Swanson, was more like something an extravagant author had written rather than a real person. He was an Austrian who supposedly graduated from the military academy in his native country. He came to the United States about 1913 and loved to tell about the menial jobs he took to keep from starving.

In an interview he claimed to have walked out to the Griffith studio in 1916 every day for two months without finding work. One day he saw John Emerson in evening dress with a ribbon across his chest. Von Stroheim claimed he told Emerson that he was wearing it incorrectly. Having intimate knowledge of the Austrian court, Von Stroheim said, he was familiar with decorations.

Emerson was impressed and offered Von Stroheim a part in *In Old Heidelberg (The Student Prince).* He played other parts for Triangle and when World War I started he cashed in on his Teutonic appearance playing German villains.

In the meantime he had written a play called *The Pinnacle,* but had no success in getting it produced. Motion picture producers were equally unimpressed with it. The story involved an American businessman who was too busy to care for his wife and how she drifted to a rascally foreigner.

Hearing that Laemmle was in Hollywood from the New York office, Von Stroheim interrupted him at dinner to try and sell *The Pinnacle.* Laemmle agreed to produce the picture and let Von Stroheim both direct and take the star role.

Big U officials were flabbergasted. They had seen the script. In their eyes, it was impossible and Von Stroheim with his arrogant manner was worse in person than his script. The truth is that Laemmle had paid scant attention to the script or the story as Von Stroheim told it. Von Stroheim was accepted solely because he spoke German to Uncle Carl. Laemmle loved Germany and had been brokenhearted when the war began. After the end of the war he was the first to suggest that Germans be forgiven and aided. He personally gave considerable sums to aid people in his old home town.

Whether Von Stroheim deliberately spoke German to interest the old man or whether he figured Laemmle could understand the proposition better if presented in his native tongue, Von Stroheim never said. Anyway, Laemmle readily agreed to make the kind of picture he had refused in the past. Furthermore, he ignored reports that Von Stroheim was wasting money.

Von Stroheim with Maude George in the 1919 film, *The Devil's Passkey.*

The picture appeared as *Blind Husbands* and was the greatest critical success Universal had made to this time. It was also popular with the public, but did not make as much money as it should have

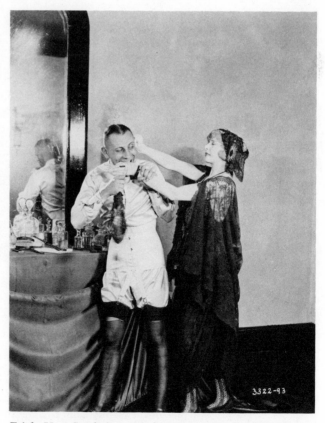

Erich Von Stroheim with Mae Busch in *Foolish Wives,* a film that incensed censors in many states.

because of Von Stroheim's extravagance in production.

After the success of *Blind Husbands* Von Stroheim had no trouble getting Universal's backing for *The Devil's Passkey*. It was also a success, but was even more expensive than *Blind Husbands*. His next picture, *Foolish Wives,* was another critical and financial success when released in 1922.

Von Stroheim had an amazing talent and an equally amazing lack of discipline. In a profession built on arrogance, he was the prince of them all. Not even Griffith with his colossal ego could top Von Stroheim in his regard for his own work. As an actor, and a superb one, he could take orders, but as a director he was absolutely incapable of understanding any viewpoint but his own. He seemed to feel that studio bosses, actors, and especially the company treasurer were in a conspiracy against him.

It was inevitable that he should come to grief. The man who first slapped him down professionally was Irving Thalberg, later the "boy genius" of Metro-Goldwyn-Mayer.

Thalberg was with Universal from 1919 to 1923. Worshipful biographers have written in awed terms of how he improved the poor quality of Universal films and brought some order out of the chaos of the studio during his four years with Big U. Actually only three pictures made during his

"Gentleman Jim," the famed James J. Corbett, conqueror of the mighty John L. Sullivan, was the big attraction in the 1919 serial, *The Midnight Man*. James Horne directed. Corbett is on the motorcycle.

regime as studio manager stood out above the regular program fare. They were *Foolish Wives, Merry-Go-Round,* and *The Hunchback of Notre Dame.* All he had to do with *Foolish Wives* was to complain of Von Stroheim's extravagance. He had more to do with *Merry-Go-Round.* He fired Von Stroheim and gave the picture to Rupert Julian to finish. The *Hunchback* was something else. This truly great film was Thalberg's idea from the beginning and he struggled to give it the kind of production that the idea deserved.

Irving Thalberg was born in Brooklyn, New York, on May 30, 1899. He was a sickly baby and child, adored by a domineering mother. In 1918, through his mother's appeal to Carl Laemmle, he went to work as an assistant to Laemmle's secretary at 1600 Broadway in New York. At this time it was considered highly improper for a businessman to travel with a woman secretary. So male secretaries were in demand. One of Thalberg's jobs was to sit beside Laemmle and take notes during screening of Big U films. The discussion that went on during these screenings gave young Thalberg an insight into motion pictures he could have gotten so quickly in no other way. Except when he made his annual trip to Germany, Laemmle saw every Big U picture. Some he saw in the projection room in the Mecca Building and some he saw in his private projection room in his home. (On summer nights he had a habit of showing them on the lawn of his home for the neighbors to see.)

Thalberg thought the pictures trite and poorly done. He especially was caustic about some chapters of *The Midnight Man,* a 1919 serial. Laemmle waved away his secretary's remarks, retorting, "But it has *Corbett.*" This was James J. Corbett, the prizefighter who years before knocked out the legendary John L. Sullivan. As time went on Thalberg kept making suggestions to which Laemmle paid little attention.

However, Uncle Carl was observing Thalberg more than the young man knew. In 1920, after Thalberg was with Universal for a year, Laemmle took him to Hollywood on a trip. Thalberg was delighted. Back in New York with the brass of the company he was just a secretary, but in Hollywood he was played up to as a man close to the big boss. This fed Thalberg's ego, which was considerable although he kept it in better control than Von Stroheim. One who didn't treat him as

somebody important was fun-loving Priscilla Dean, who didn't treat anyone with respect. She was then making *The Virgin of Stamboul* under Tod Browning's direction. It was the story of a spitfire beggar girl who finally marries an Englishman. Miss Dean, fast becoming the most important female star at Big U, evidently got carried away with the role, for she married the hero, Wheeler Oakman, both on and off the screen.

Priscilla Dean romped through Tod Browning's *The Virgin of Stamboul,* made in 1920.

When Laemmle went back to New York he left Thalberg as the West Coast studio manager. This stunned everyone, for Thalberg was twenty-one years old (and not nineteen as he is often stated to be). Thalberg's only training for the job was the year he had spent as a male secretary in the New York office. The peculiar choice was put down to Uncle Carl's increasing eccentricity. It is more likely that Laemmle had something else in mind. Studio managers had seldom taken a hand in actual filmmaking. H. O. Davis had given

107

Irving Thalberg got to know Clarence Brown when both worked for Universal. Brown directed *The Goose Woman* for Universal in 1925.

producers (actually directors) set budgets. They were then expected to make a saleable picture within these monetary limitations. The director usually picked the story, cast the film, and made the picture.

In this kind of set-up there wasn't a lot for Thalberg to do, Laemmle figured. The young man was already paying court to Laemmle's pretty daughter, Rosabelle, and for a time it looked serious. Uncle Carl, with his well known paternalism, was just taking care of a future relative and building Thalberg up. However, the expected wedding never came off.

Thalberg was a different type from H. O. Davis. He began to meddle in production. He wanted to approve stories, casts, and budgets in advance. Of course, in a film factory like Big U, it was impossible for him to oversee every picture. He concentrated on the features and let the comedies and two-reelers pretty much take care of themselves.

10 Dean, Denny, and the Hunchback

Thalberg was not liked at Universal. Directors, used to having their way, resented his interference. The legion of Laemmle relatives thought that one of them should have been given the positon. As a result, directors and stars began moving on. Dorothy Phillips and Alan Holubar left. After Pat Powers sold his interest in Universal to Laemmle and Cochrane, Harry Carey went with Powers as soon as his contract ran out in 1921. Mae Murray and Robert Z. Leonard left. John Ford also left after making *Sure Fire*, with Hoot Gibson and Molly Malone in 1921.

On the other hand, Thalberg got along famously with some of his temperamental employees. Rupert Julian was quite fond of him. So was Tod Browning. Thalberg, better than H. O. Davis or Laemmle, recognized Browning's talent. He encouraged Browning to put more money into production values and the quality of Browning's films for Universal in 1920 and 1921 showed this increased attention.

There had been an economic let-down after the close of World War I and business was not as good as it might have been. Also, Universal had slipped in the last few years. In 1912 the name of the New Universal stood for quality films, and top stars. In 1920 it had neither star nor picture to match what other studios were presenting. This was the year Charlie Chaplin released *The Kid*, Mary Pickford made *Pollyana*, Fairbanks swung his swashbuckling sword in *The Mark of Zorro*, Griffith turned out *Way Down East*, First National showed Ernst Lubitsch's German production of *Passion*, with Pola Negri, ex-Universalite Mae Murrey made *On With the Dance* at Paramount, Tom Mix was riding high at Fox, Pauline Frederick made *Madame X* for Goldwyn, Wallace Reid was at the top at Paramount, De Mille was creating a legend of Gloria Swanson, John Barrymore made *Dr. Jekyll and Mr. Hyde*, Frank Borzage (another Universal alumni) made *Humoresque* to critical applause, Jack Mulhall and Betty Compson were doing well away from Big U, and Lon Chaney — fresh from his 1919 triumph in the Mayflower Production of *The Miracle Man* — made *The Penalty* for Goldwyn.

Against these crowd-pleasers Thalberg had only Priscilla Dean as a real star. Others were standing in the wings of fame waiting their opportunity, but they had not yet reached the heights. They included such men as Frank Mayo, Norman Kerry, and Reginald Denny. Among the women were Mary Philbin, Laura La Plante and Gladys Walton. Later Herbert Rawlinson returned and Hoot Gibson developed into a drawing card second only to Tom Mix and Buck Jones in the western field.

It is rather difficult to assess Priscilla Dean's appeal. She was pretty, but no beauty. When you ask old-timers what they saw in her, the answer is invariably, "It was the kind of pictures she made." And these were right in the groove of the *My Lady Raffles* series that Grace Cunard made.

In *Reputation*, 1921, directed by Stuart Paton, she played an actress who abandons her child. She

Eddie Lyons and Lee Moran were a comedy team at Universal for almost ten years. Moran was a friend of Lon Chaney and got "The Man of a Thousand Faces" his first job with Universal. *Fixed By George*, a two-reel comedy, was released in 1920.

develops into a dope fiend and as the years pass gets so bad that her manager replaces her with a young girl. In a rage Priscilla shoots the manager. The young actress is blamed. Then when the older woman learns that the accused is really the daughter she abandoned, she confesses.

Miss Dean's big hits in 1921 were *Under Two Flags* and *Outside the Law*. The role of Cigarette was made to order for her. "Cigarette — born in the shadow of a cannon, the tri-color her quilt, her mother an Arab and her father a Frenchman, what can you expect of her?"

The audience expected a dazzling performance and got it. *Under Two Flags* is the famous novel by the Victorian writer Ouida (Marie Louise de la Ramee). It is the story of Bertie Cecil, who takes

the blame for a crime he didn't do and joins the French Foreign Legion in Algiers. He meets Cigarette, who is a wild half-breed orphan, a pet of the regiment. She falls in love with the handsome Englishman, but he loves the Princess Corona d'Amague, an Englishwoman who is the widow of a Frenchman. Bertie's brother, who has inherited the title after their father's death, is touring Algiers. He is dismayed to find his older brother and the rightful heir still living. After the colonel of the regiment insults the princess, Bertie strikes him and is sentenced to death. Cigarette goes to see the field marshal and gets a stay of execution, but the colonel refuses to accept it. His honor has been wounded. Cigarette throws herself in front of Bertie and takes the bullets intended for him.

In *Reputation*, 1921, Priscilla Dean played a drug-sodden actress whose daughter, also played by Miss Dean, took her mother's role on the stage. Stuart Paton directed.

Once each generation someone has to remake Ouida's famous novel *Under Two Flags.* In 1921 it was Priscilla Dean's time to play Cigarette, the sweetheart of a French Foreign Legion regiment, who have her life for the man she loved. Tod Browning directed.

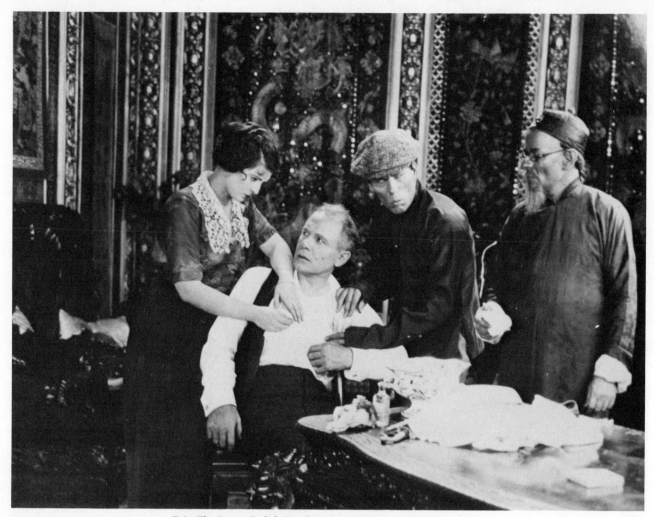

Priscilla Dean, Ralph Lewis, Lon Chaney, and E. A. Warren
in Tod Browning's *Outside the Law*, 1921.

Bertie is released to marry the princess and return to England to claim his title, but he never forgets Cigarette.

Outside the Law was made by Tod Browning. It was the best of his Universal pictures until he returned in the talkie era to make *Dracula*. It was the idea he told Chaney he was working on when he released Lon to accept the role of Frog in *The Miracle Man.* It starred Priscilla Dean in her familiar role of a lady crook who reformed in the final reel.

In the story Silent Madden (Ralph Lewis) and his daughter, Silky Moll, decide to quit their life of crime. The gang leader Mike Silva (Lon Chaney) frames Madden, who goes to prison for shooting an officer. Silky Moll, enraged by her father's unjust sentence, returns to her life of crime. She teams with Dapper Dan (Wheeler Oakman). Silva, hating Moll, orders Dan to take Moll with him on a jewel robbery. After she gets the jewels, Dan is to take them and leave her to take the blame.

But Dan and Moll fall in love and the two escape together from the robbery scene. They hide in a hotel to escape both Silva and the police. Chang Lo (E. A. Warren), a friend of Madden, gets the victim of the robbery to promise to drop charges if the gems are returned. Chang Lo then sends his servant Ah Wing (Lon Chaney) to persuade Dan and Moll to return the jewels.

Before they can do so, Silva finds them. He attempts to kill both Dan and Moll, but is killed himself by Ah Wing. Madden is released from jail

112

when it is revealed that Silva shot the officer. Moll and Dan are married.

Chaney, playing the roles of Silva and Ah Wing, created considerable comment for the scene — a double exposure — in which he shot himself.

The 1923 film *Drifting* is a typical example of Priscilla Dean's pictures. She is a dope smuggler in China, pursued by an undercover man, Tom Moore. She reforms and marries her pursuer.

Seeking a male matinee idol to replace J. Warren Kerrigan, who had been Universal's most popular star before World War I, Universal signed Frank Mayo, the third generation of his family to act under that name. He made his debut at the age of four in his grandfather's most famous play, *Davy Crockett.* He claimed that while he was on

Lon Chaney gave two outstanding performances in *Outside the Law,* playing both the gangster, Mike Silva, above and Ah Wing, the Chinese who shoots Silva.

stage rehearsing this part his mother sat in a box watching and sewing him a little coonskin cap to wear in the play. After achieving manhood, he went to England where he made his first film, working for the London Film Company in 1914 with Edna Flugrath, sister of Viola Dana and Shirley Mason, under George Loane Tucker.

Back in the United States he played leads with Alice Brady at World and Ethel Clayton at Paramount before Universal signed him to replace J. Warren Kerrigan. He was a far handsomer man than Kerrigan, but instead of romantic leads, Universal cast him in fighting adventure films.

In *The Throwback,* 1921, he played a Fairbanks-type role of a worthless young clubman who goes to South America to manage a rubber plantation. Here, away from civilization, he reverts to a pioneer type whose fists play havoc with heavies out to destroy the plantation.

In *The Sharkmaster,* also 1921, he played a man shipwrecked on a desert island. The plot is, except for a happy instead of a sad ending, almost identical to the 1912 Kalem picture *A Tragedy of the Desert.* Thinking he will never be rescued, he marries a native girl. Then a ship with his old fiancée appears. In the Kalem film the native wife, seeing her husband with the other woman, thinks he is leaving and kills herself. In this one Mayo chooses to stay with the native girl.

On the feminine side the big newcomer was Gladys Walton, a Cinderella type who illustrates the casual way people become film actors in those days. In 1920 Miss Walton graduated from high school in Portland, Oregon, and her mother brought her seventeen-year-old daughter to Los Angeles for a visit. Gladys decided she would try to get in the movies just to have something to tell her friends when she got back to Portland. She didn't expect to make it and was surprised when Fox accepted her. Her pretty legs were what did it. They wanted her for the Sunshine Girls, Fox's equivalent of Sennett's Bathing Beauties.

After a few weeks at Fox she applied to Universal. They also recognized her chief attraction. She was placed in films about circus performers, ballet dancers, and the like where she could be costumed to show her legs. An exception is *Crossed Wires,* where she was a telephone operator who overheard plans for a society party and invited herself to attend.

The Man Tamer was more typical of her

Anna May Wong reveals to undercover agent Tom Moore
that Priscilla Dean is not so innocent after all in this scene
from *Drifting,* 1923.

Frank Mayo was hired as a romantic fighting type to
replace J. Warren Kerrigan. Here he is in *The Sharkmaster,*
1921.

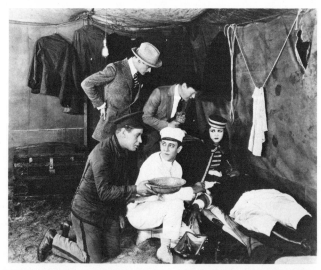

Gladys Walton (as Kitty) finds her father (Rex Rosselli) dying. C. B. Murphy holds the pan and directly behind the man in white is Roscoe Karns. The picture is the 1921 *The Man Tamer.*

pictures. In this one she was Kitty Horrigan who assists her father in a lion tamer act. Her father (Rex Roselli) is killed and Kitty is forced to leave the circus to escape the lecherous owner, Delmar (William Welch). Loyal Tim Murphy (C. B. Murphy), an animal handler, goes with her. She meets rich Bradley Caldwell, Jr., who has seen her act and has fallen in love with her. Caldwell, Jr., is constantly being arrested for wild escapades. He needs, everyone says, taming.

He keeps pursuing a reluctant Kitty until he is gradually tamed by her, renouncing his wild ways. Still she refuses to marry him. He leaves, vowing to change her mind eventually. She is then visited by Caldwell, Senior, who says he has learned that Junior has proposed to her. He says that under no circumstances will he permit his son to marry a mere lion tamer. Kitty, enraged, tells him off and runs out. Junior goes to find her and discovers that the circus owner, Delmar, has kidnapped Kitty by the use of hypnotism learned from a Hindu swami with the circus. Junior and Tim rush to her rescue. They arrive just in time to prevent what writers of that day characterized "a fate worse than death." Kitty falls in Junior's arms. He repeats his proposal. She tells him what his father told her. Junior laughed. "He was trying to help me," he said. "Father thinks you did a wonderful job as a 'man tamer.' When I told him you had turned me down, he said he had learned in his sixty-five years

that the way to make a woman do something was to tell her she couldn't do it! So he did!"

And they, presumably, lived happily ever after. And so did seventeen-year-old Gladys, who got married herself.

While Priscilla Dean and Frank Mayo held the center stage at the beginning of the twenties, three new stars were beginning to glow and in a very short time they would be the top three at Universal. They were Hoot Gibson, Laura La Plante, and Reginald Denny.

Hoot was no newcomer. He had been around for a long time. He was originally a rodeo rider, making what he could by riding bucking horses. In the course of following the rodeo circuit he met and married Helen Rose Wenger, who was also a rodeo rider. Hoot was very good and once won the All-Around Cowboy title at the Pendleton Round-up.

In time they wandered to Hollywood where they heard riders could pick up good money riding

In 1925 Hoot Gibson made *Chip of the Flying U,* one of his most successful films. Here Hoot violates western movie tradition by wearing a black hat, which was supposed to be reserved for the bad guys in films.

in westerns. They worked first for Ince and then for Kalem. When Helen Holmes left with her husband J. P. McGowan to join Universal, Helen Gibson, who had been doubling for Helen Holmes, succeeded to Miss Holmes's role in the endless series *The Hazards of Helen,* a group of railroad stories. Hoot played bit parts and supporting roles in his wife's films. After she moved to Universal in 1916, Hoot came along and picked up what work he could get.

In late 1916 Hoot was noticed by Jack Ford, who gave him parts in several Harry Carey films, all of which were released in 1917. The first was *The Soul Herder.* Then he played a background cowboy in *Cheyenne's Pal,* a gunman in *Straight Shooting,* a sheriff in *A Marked Man,* and a bit role in *The Secret Man.*

Then when the United States entered World War I in April 1917, Edward "Hoot" Gibson was among the first to enlist. After serving in France, he came back to Universal in 1919, where Jack Ford put him into *The Fighting Brothers* with Pete Morrison. This was Hoot's best role to date. He played the younger brother of Sheriff Larkin (Pete Morrison), who is accused of murder. The sheriff, bound by duty, arrests Lonnie (Hoot) and sees him taken to prison. Then the sheriff turns in his badge and goes out to get Lonnie out of jail.

After this film, Hoot began getting better roles. In *Gun Law,* 1919, he played a mail bandit sought by Pete Morrison. The search is complicated by Morrison falling in love with Gibson's sister, played by Helen Gibson, and then by Gibson saving Morrison's life. Morrison then put love and friendship before duty.

Hoot still tried to make the big rodeos, like the Pendleton Oregon Roundup and the Calgary, Canada, Stampede. The publicity this brought, plus his engaging personality and genuine riding ability, helped him develop a following. Other directors picked him up and he had leading roles in the last two pictures Ford made for Universal before moving to Fox in 1921.

He was penciled in for a role in *Desperate Trails* with Harry Carey, Irene Rich, and — of all people to be in a western — Barbara La Marr, but an injury kept him out of the cast. Ford then used him for the lead in *Action,* a picture so good that it was marketed as a Universal-Special. The story was about three range bums who kept the bad guys from stealing the Three Star Ranch belonging to orphan Clara Horton. Francis Ford returned to

Big U to play one of the three. This was a considerable comedown for a man who had been the biggest male draw on the lot only four years before.

Hoot's next picture, and Jack Ford's last for Universal, was *Sure Fire,* 1921, which was based on a Eugene Manlove Rhodes story.

From this point on Edward "Hoot" Gibson never looked back. He rode at breakneck speed right into the top ranks of western stars, a position he held through the remainder of the silent era.

Laura LaPlante, who would be Big U's most important actress in the last half of the 1920s, was born in St. Louis, Missouri, in 1905. She moved to San Diego as a child and decided at that time that she would be a movie actress. At fourteen she applied to the Al Christie Studio for work. Christie, who had made Nestor Comedies for Universal, left Big U in 1916 to produce independently with his brother as partner. Laura worked for Christie for four years and then moved to Universal in 1922. She worked her way up through

Relaticity, 1922, was one of Laura La Plante's early Universal features. With her, from left, are Frances Raymond, Lucille Ricksen, Jennie Lee, Laura La Plante, and veteran Lydia Yeamans Titus.

supporting roles to the climax of her career as Magnolia in the first filming of *Showboat,* released by Universal in 1929.

She played in Westerns and in a picture called *Relaticity* in 1922 before hitting her stride as the love interest in Reginald Denny's comedy features.

Reginald Denny first found fame as the cultured boxer in *Leather Pushers* series. Hayden Stevenson played the manager.

Denny was the best of the light comedians and in many ways took the place of Wallace Reid in the public's affection after that tragic actor died as a result of dope addiction. Many of Denny's Universal films were written by Byron Morgan, who had written some of Wallace Reid's best films. However, Denny had a better comic sense than Reid and was perfectly matched with his director, William A. Seiter.

Seiter was born in 1892. After attending the Hudson River Military Academy he became an artist and writer. This led him to join Selig and then Reliance before accepting an offer to direct comedy for Universal. He married Laura La Plante in 1926.

Denny was born in 1894 in Surrey, England, the son of W. H. Denny, who had played with Gilbert and Sullivan. He made his own debut at the age of five at the Court Theater in London. He came to the United States with a touring company in 1911, but returned to England and then went to India with a musical comedy company. He had a very good baritone voice. He enlisted in the Royal Flying Corps in 1917 and won the brigade's heavyweight boxing championship. After the war he came back to New York and then went to work for Oscar Apfel (who co-directed *The Squaw Man* with Cecil B. DeMille). One of his films for Apfel was *The Oakdale Affair,* from a story by Edgar Rice Burroughs, the author of *Tarzan.* It was released in 1918. He then played on the stage with John Barrymore in *Richard III* and made several other pictures, including *Footlights* with Elsie Ferguson.

His big break came in 1922, but it didn't appear to be one at the time. A small company was

The company went broke and Universal took over and finished the series. They were so popular, under the series name, *The Leather Pushers,* that Denny made a second series.

In one of the films he anticipated Gorgeous George, the wrestler, by appearing in the ring in an

Eva Novak, sister of the more famous Jane Novak, starred
in *The Torrent* in 1920.

formed to film a two-reel series based upon some boxing short stories H. C. Witwer was writing in *Colliers* magazine. They dealt with an educated young man who becomes a boxer to restore the family fortune lost by his father. Denny was cast as Kid Robertson and Hayden Stevenson was his manager.

embroidered dressing gown and had a liveried footman serve him tea in his corner.

At the end of the third series, Denny had become so popular that Universal couldn't afford to waste him on two-reelers anymore. He was moved to features, first under Harry Pollard and then with Bill Seiter. His place in *The Leather*

Pushers was taken by Billy Sullivan, a nephew of the great fighter John L. Sullivan.

Others who were forging ahead were Jane and Eva Novak, sisters from St. Louis, Missouri, Virginia Valli, the Sedgwicks (Edward the director, his sisters Eileen and Josephine), and Wallace Beery.

Beery had acted and directed for Universal in 1916 and 1917 and then left to freelance. He did remarkably well, especially after Thomas H. Ince cast him with Hobart Bosworth in *Behind the Door.* Then his hit performance as Richard the Lionhearted in Douglas Fairbanks's *Robin Hood* in 1922 assured his future. He was in tremendous demand at all the studios and always had five or six roles waiting for him. Those who remember Beery as the lovable old scamp of his later pictures do not know what a marvelously versatile actor he was.

In the meantime, Von Stroheim's *Foolish Wives* ran into censor trouble. He bragged to an interviewer that he spent one million four hundred thousand dollars on the film and that it made back the production costs in four months. In railing against the censors, he told a reporter for *Classic* magazine: "My ears have run with their united cry: 'It is not fit for children!' Children! Children! God! I did not make that picture for children. I had not one thought for children, any more than Hugo, or Voltaire, or Shakespeare, or any writer of intelligence and sincerity, had thought for children."

He went on to insist that if a law was not passed barring children from attendance at motion picture theaters, "then the movie industry will die." After this outburst he complained of the personal hatred of himself.

"Because of my attempt at sincerity, I have been condemned, hooted at, reviled; filthy rumors have been circulated about me . . . . They never say 'Count Karamzin, the beast [the character in *Foolish Wives*]!' They say, 'Von Stroheim, the beast!' Why?"

He ended up by saying, "I am told to think only of money. The heart is taken from me, and I am still expected to go on. Very well, I shall. I can. I will."

His next film was the famous *Merry-Go-Round,* laid in Vienna with Norman Kerry as the lecherous seducer in pursuit of virginal Mary Philbin. Von Stroheim had wanted to play the Kerry role himself, but Thalberg refused. Then when Von Stroheim surpassed his previous extravagance,

Thalberg fired him from the picture. Rupert Julian, who was often as temperamental as Von Stroheim, but not nearly so extravagant, was given the picture to finish. When it was released in 1923, it carried Julian's name as director. There was no mention of Von Stroheim.

Norman Kerry seduces Mary Philbin in the 1923 film *Merry-Go-Round,* from which Thalberg fired Von Stroheim and gave to Rupert Julian to complete.

Thalberg's own days at Universal were limited. His romance with Rosabelle had ended and the Laemmle relatives were loading Uncle Carl with complaints about Thalberg's high-handedness. Thalberg himself was dissatisfied with his inability to fire most of the incompetent relatives and by the smallness of his salary. He was getting $450 a week and thought he should get a thousand.

Thalberg began looking for a new position. Thalberg's biographer, Bob Thomas, claims that Thalberg found a job with Louis B. Mayer and that Uncle Carl was very angry at the loss. There is considerable evidence that Uncle Carl was pleased to get rid of Thalberg whom he hated to fire. It is doubtful, however, that he actually asked Mayer "to take that young man off my hands," as another writer claimed. He and Mayer had never had any use for each other.

Before Thalberg left in February 1923 he set in motion a project that would be the crowning glory of Universal's silent years. This was *The Hunchback of Notre Dame,* based upon an adaption by

119

Lon Chaney reached his peak as Quasimodo, *The Hunch-back of Notre Dame*, in the 1923 film with Patsy Ruth Miller.

Perley Poore Sheehan of Victor Hugo's classic novel, *Notre Dame de Paris*.

This film was Thalberg's idea from the beginning. He saw it in epic terms and sold Laemmle on letting him go ahead with it on a larger-than-normal budget. Thalberg had Lon Chaney in mind for the role of Quasimodo, the hunchback, from the beginning, but had difficulty selecting a director. A note in *Motion Picture News* in 1922 said that he was searching for the proper man to direct Chaney in the role. He was considering Rupert Julian, but decided against it because of his trouble with Von Stroheim. He wanted Julian free to take over *Merry-Go-Round* if it became necessary to fire the arrogant Austrian, which it did.

While the sets were being constructed and Thalberg vascillated over a director, Chaney agreed to make *The Shock*, one of his few romantic leads. Several things about it appealed to Chaney. It was to be directed by Lambert Hillyer, who had been behind the megaphone on *Riddle Gawne*, Chaney's first free-lance film after leaving Universal in 1918. It cast Chaney in a sympathetic role, and it had a San Francisco earthquake climax as had *Hell Morgan's Girl*.

Chaney played Wilse Dilling, a cripple, who was sent to blackmail a man hated by "Queen Anne," a woman gang leader played by Christine Mayo. Chaney falls in love with the man's daughter, played by Virginia Valli. He doublecrosses the gang and Queen Anne has the girl kidnapped. Wilse drags himself to the saloon where she is imprisoned and the building collapses in the earthquake. He saves the girl. The shock, plus his love for her, cures his affliction and they presumably live happily ever after.

Thalberg talked to Chaney who suggested Wallace Worsley to direct *The Hunchback.* Thalberg had been considering Robert T. Thornby, who had directed Chaney in *The Trap,* a Universal Jewel release in 1921. This picture, with Alan Hale, Irene Rich, and Dagmar Godowsky, received exceptional reviews for the dramatic climax in which Chaney fights a wolf with his bare hands to

save the child (Stanley Goethals) of his enemy from death in a trap Chaney has set for the boy's father, Alan Hale.

The scene was played in a dark room broken by a single shaft of moonlight from a window so that the audience only glimpsed Chaney and the wolf at intervals. Critics called it an imaginative and extremely dramatic scene.

However, after borrowing and running Worsley's Goldwyn film, *The Penalty,* with Chaney, Thalberg agreed on Wallace Worsley. In *The Penalty* Chaney played a legless man intent upon killing his enemy whom he blamed for the loss of his legs. The picture was so skillfully directed and acted that

Lon Chaney, center foreground, reaches to aid Virginia Valli in the climactic earthquake scene in *The Shock,* a 1923 film directed by Lambert Hillyer. This was one of the few films in which Chaney played a romantic lead.

121

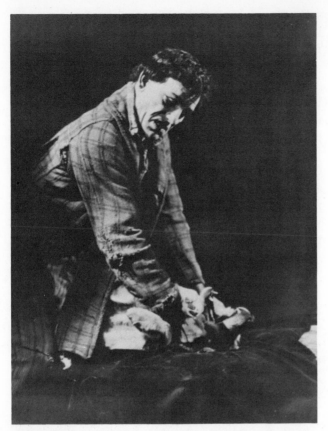

The climactic scene in the 1922 film, *The Trap,* where Lon Chaney fights a wolf barehanded, was greatly praised for the direction by Robert T. Thornby.

whelming. The public for once agreed with the critics. There was some critical carping about Chaney's makeup, which some thought overdone, but opinion was unanimous about Ernest Torrence's work as the beggar chieftan. Some thought him better than Chaney. Modern audiences do not get much chance to evaluate Torrence's performance. The original picture was twelve reels. It was cut after the initial roadshow at inflated prices and some of the modern versions seen today on television and old-time movie theaters have been cut even more.

For some time Laemmle had been fighting roadshows and special priced films, claiming that they were robbing exhibitors and the public. Now faced with the necessity of doing the same in order to recoup the heavy expense of *The Hunchback,* he stuck to his guns in denouncing the entire idea, but insisted in one broadside to exhibitors that only two pictures in the history of films deserved special price treatment. One, he said, was *The Covered Wagon* (which Paramount released in 1923) and the other was *The Hunchback of Notre Dame.*

There had been some uneasiness in Catholic circles about the film when it was first announced. The original Hugo novel was written to expose abysmal social conditions in fifteenth-century France. The venality of the priesthood was one of the points Victor Hugo attacked.

Perley Poore Sheehan's adaptation skirted these

sympathy was aroused for the villainous Blizzard. This was exactly what Thalberg wanted in *The Hunchback.*

"I want the audience to slowly grow to love this repulsive beast of a man," he said. And in Chaney and chubby, be-spectacled Wallace Worsley he found the team to give him what he wanted.

Thalberg helped by giving Worsley a tremendous cast that included Raymond Hatton, Gladys Brockwell, Ernest Torrence, Norman Kerry, and Patsy Ruth Miller, plus hundreds of extras for the mob scenes. The sets, including the Notre Dame cathedral and the Paris streets, were superb.

Thalberg was not around to see the picture finished. He resigned in February 1923 to join Louis B. Mayer Productions as Vice-President in charge of Production. He was succeeded at Universal by a man named Koenig. The picture was released September 16, 1923. Chaney made a trip to New York to be present at the premiere.

Critical success of *The Hunchback* was over-

Irving Thalberg spared no expense in providing exceptional production values for *The Hunchback of Notre Dame.* Here one of the sets is under construction.

122

Estelle Taylor, Forrest Stanley, and Wallace Beery engage in
Russian intrigue in the 1923 film *Bavu*.

controversial points. He considerably altered the
story, making the real villain Jehan, the brother of
the priest, Dom Claude. Brandon Hurst played
Jehan and Nigel de Brulier was the priest.

In Sheehan's version Jehan covets Esmeralda
(Patsy Ruth Miller) and sends the brutish, mis-
shapen hunchback, Quasimodo, the deaf bell ringer
of Notre Dame cathedral, to kidnap the girl for
him. She is the ward of Clopin, king of Parisian
theives. Captain Phoebus (Norman Kerry) rescues
her and Quasimodo is sentenced to a public
whipping. His brutish heart is touched when after
the beating she brings him water to drink.

Later Jehan stabs Captain Phoebus and
Esmeralda is accused. She is tried and condemned.
She is then taken to Notre Dame to ask God's
forgiveness before she is executed. Quasimodo sees
her from the bell tower. He slides down a rope

(doubled by Joe Bonomo), grabs Esmeralda, and
disappears into the cathedral. The cathedral is a
"place of refuge" and the soldiers cannot follow.

Clopin arouses a beggar army and attacks the
cathedral to get Esmeralda. Quasimodo hurls a
beam and then molten lead down upon them. This
holds them at bay until Capt Phoebus, partially
recovered from Jehan's stabbing, arrives with his
soldiers to scatter the thieves.

Quasimodo rushes back to his room where he
left Esmeralda. She has been stolen by Jehan.
Quasimodo follows and catches them on the roof
of the cathedral. He hurls Jehan over the parapet,
but not before the evil man stabs the hunchback.
Quasimodo dies as Esmeralda and Captain Phoebus
are reunited.

In the original Hugo story, the hunchback and
Esmeralda disappear. Years later workmen

Wallace Beery, despite the pleas of his film daughter,
Priscilla Dean, fights his mine foreman, Robert Ellis,
because Ellis fired him for smoking in the coal mine, in the
1923 film *The Flame of Life.*

The White Tiger, 1923, featured Priscilla Dean and Wallace
Beery in a continuation of the popular "crook" roles Miss
Dean did so well.

uncovering a forgotten cell in the cathedral find two skeletons. One of a girl and one of a man with a crooked spine.

Merry-Go-Round and *The Hunchback of Notre Dame* overshadowed all the other pictures of Universal's 1923 releases, but Wallace Beery, supported by Estelle Taylor and Forrest Stanley, turned in a highly rated performance as the Russian revolutionist in *Bavu,* directed by Stuart Paton. Beery turned in another superb performance with Priscilla Dean in *The White Tiger.* They also appeared together in *The Flame of Life.*

Jack Conway, a Minnesota boy who came to the movies after working with Belasco, was already at twenty-six showing some of the promise that made him a top MGM director later. He megaphoned Gladys Walton in *Sawdust* in 1923.

Frank Mayo, his contract expiring after *The Bolted Door,* bolted himself, moving to Metro in hope he could get better stories.

On the western range Hoot Gibson's star was rising fast. In quick order he made *Single-Handed, Dead Game* (in which he was billed as Edward Gibson), *Double Dealing, Shooting For Love, Out of Luck,* and *Blinky.*

In *Blinky* he played a worthless society youth whose disgusted father, a retired army colonel, used influence to get Blinky placed with the father's old cavalry regiment. He has to take a lot of rawhiding from members of the troop, but when the commandant's daughter is kidnapped, it is Blinky who proves himself a true son of old "Raw Meat" Inslip and rescues the girl (Esther Ralston). Edward Sedgwick directed from a story by Gene Markey.

Art Acord, who had been around Hollywood since the days of the New York Motion Picture Company, made two Western serials for Big U. One was *Winners of the West* in 1921 with Myrtle Lind and ZaSu Pitts, and *In the Days of Buffalo Bill* in 1922 with Dorothy Woods. Some other serials of this period were *The Adventures of Robinson Crusoe,* 1922, with Harry Myers and Noble Johnson, *Perils of the Yukon,* 1922, with William Desmond and Laura La Plante, and *The Eagle's Talons* with Fred Thompson, Ann Little, and Joe Bonomo.

Other serials were *With Stanley in Africa,* 1922, with George Walsh and Louise Lorraine; *Around the World in 18 Days,* 1923, with William Desmond and Laura La Plante; *The Ghost City,* 1923, with Pete Morrison and Margaret Morris (a western despite its name); *The Oregon Trail* with Art Acord and Louise Lorraine; and *The Steel Trail* with William Duncan and Edith Johnson.

Duncan was an athlete from Scotland who had appeared in early Selig movies. He moved to Vitagraph where he made a series of highly successful serials with his wife, Edith Johnson, as co-star. Vitagraph was running into financial trouble and Duncan thought it expedient to change companies. Universal gave him complete control of his own unit. Duncan played a construction engineer beset by troubles in building a railroad.

Although serials were supposedly dropping in popularity, Big U released seven in 1923.

In the straight feature drama field, Herbert Rawlinson returned to Universal. Milton Sills made *Legally Dead* and played with Virginia Valli in her starring picture, *A Lady of Quality.* and Baby Peggy graduated from two-reels comedies to her first feature, *The Darling of New York.* Baby Peggy Montgomery was an especially winsome three-year

Art Acord, Myrtle Lind, and ZaSu Pitts in Edward Laemmle's 1921 serial *Winners of the West.*

125

Old-time western fans have fond memories of Art Acord, seen here in a beautiful still from *In the Days of Buffalo Bill*. The girl in buckskins at his stirrup is Dorothy Woods. The eighteen-chapter serial was directed by Edward Laemmle and released in 1922.

Harry Myers and Joe Martin, the ape, share the loneliness of *The Adventures of Robinson Crusoe*, the 1922 serial.

Perils of the Yukon, the 1922 serial, was William Desmond's introduction to the serial field. Here he is with Harry Carter and Laura La Plante.

Ann Little, Al Wilson, Joe Bonomo, Fred Thompson, and Fred Kohler in the 1923 serial *The Eagle's Talons.* The chapter play was directed by Duke Worne. Thompson, an ex-Marine chaplain, went on to greater fame as a cowboy star for Paramount.

Peter Morrison, cowboy star, had the lead with Margaret Morris in the 1923 serial *The Ghost City.* This still is from episode 1, *The Thundering Herd.* Jay Marchant directed.

127

In 1923 William Duncan moved from Vitagraph to Universal to direct and star in *The Steel Trail,* in which he played a railroad construction engineer.

-old when she attracted attention in a Brownie (the dog) comedy for Universal's Century Company. She then made a series of pictures of her own with such titles as *Carmen Jr., Peg O' the Movies, Taking Orders, The Kid Reporter,* and *Sweetie.*

Laemmle was still plugging the "Balanced Program," and Universal obediently ground out hundreds of two-reel dramas that could be packaged together to make a full program. Pete Morrison, veteran Roy Stewart, Edward Cobb, Jack Daugherty, Reginald Denny, Neal Hart, Jack Morley, and others turned out a flood of them. In addition, Big U rereleased a number of Harry Carey's early two-reelers. One of these was the 1917 Jacques Jaccard-directed, *The Cowboy and the Lady,* with Louise Lovely.

The major newcomer in 1923 was Jack Hoxie. Hoxie was born in Oklahoma in 1890. His father was a rancher and Jack grew up in the saddle, first in Oklahoma and later in Utah. Despite his large size, he became a trick rider with a Wild West show. He also played the rodeo circuit where he was a rival of Hoot Gibson and Art Acord. Acord, incidentally, was runner-up at the Pendleton Roundup for all-around cowboy in 1912, the year Hoot Gibson won the title. Norman Kerry met Hoxie and got the cowboy a job in the movies. After his pictures began to catch on, Universal made him an offer. Hoxie moved from the quickies to Big U in 1923. His first Universal film was *Don Quickshot of the Rio Grande.*

11 The Phantom Years

The depression that followed World War I had eased by 1924 and the wild speculation in the stock market that made paper fortunes that evaporated in the 1929 crash caused booms in the motion picture industry as well. But at the same time the growth of radio and better roads and more easily obtainable transportation reduced movie audiences as a whole.

From his beginning Carl Laemmle was an independent and sold his products to independent exhibitors. As a result he was left behind in the trend toward monopoly in which the producer also controlled exhibition. Adolph Zukor, with the Paramount Publix chain; Metro-Goldwyn-Mayer, with the enormous Loew's circuit; William Fox, with his theater acquisitions; and others were sewing up the major picture houses in the key cities. Laemmle bought a few showcase theaters in the big cities, but mainly he relied on selling to independents in a market where independents were being backed to the wall.

This was also a time when producers like Thalberg at Metro-Goldwyn (not yet graced with the addition of Mayer's name), Cecil B. De Mille, Jesse L. Lasky at Paramount, and William Fox were concentrating on big pictures with big names, but Laemmle continued to produce what were mainly program pictures. Except in westerns and serials, where Universal held its own, his features boasted no stars that could compete with those being developed by Paramount, Fox and the soon-to-emerge Metro-Goldwyn-Mayer.

It was ironic that a goodly number of those whose pictures were drawing crowds that should have come to Universal exhibitors were actors and actresses who had gotten their start at Big U.

With the exception of Von Stroheim's films and the *Hunchback,* Universal failed to put enough money into pictures to satisfy the stars. They wanted to make big pictures and took the first opportunity to get to another studio. Of course, there were others like Valentino whom the powers-that-be just failed to recognize as having potential. If it had not been for Carmel Myers and Mae Murray, Rudy Valentino would never have worked for Big U.

The old order was passing. No longer were directors or stars leaders of their own companies. The familiar names such a Bison, Rex, Eclair, Victor, Laemmle, and the others dropped out of sight. Bluebird survived as a comedy company, but the other pictures were all marketed as Universal. If they were better than average, then they were called Universal Jewels. If epic in quality, such as *The Hunchback of Notre Dame,* then they were called Universal Super Jewels.

The tremendous growth of the company was shown in figures released in 1924. Laboratory production in 1909, when IMP was formed, was 5,200,000 feet a year of processed film. In 1923, this had grown to 93, 204, 124 feet.

This growth had taken away some of the original intimacy of the company. For years Laemmle viewed every picture made by Universal. An old-timer once wrote how it was in IMP days: "Every Friday was what was called a 'sample night.' That is, all the scenes that were shot during the week were printed and developed. The stars, directors, bosses, laboratory help, and everybody, passed judgment on the work . . . . I remember one kick registered by Mr. Laemmle, who wanted the wall paper in the sets changed because he was sick of seeing the same paper in every subject."

January 28, 1924 was the fiftieth anniversary of Carl Laemmle's landing in America. Paul Gulick, director of publicity for Universal, bannered February as being "Carl Laemmle Anniversary Month." All publicity for *Merry-Go-Round, Sporting Youth, Acquittal* (with Claire Windsor and Norman Kerry), Hoot Gibson's firefighting picture, *Hook and Ladder,* and other films being pushed carried the anniversary logotype.

January 1924, also marked the departure of another famous Universal star, one more difficult to replace than the Valentinos and Murrays. He was Joe Martin, variously described in Universal publicity as a monk, chimp, and an orangutan. Joe had played with Elmo Lincoln and Louise Lorraine in *The Adventures of Tarzan* for Numa Pictures in 1921, but he belonged to Universal and was used by the company in a long series of one-reel comedies, in addition to supporting any feature that required some monkey business.

An example of his art is *A White Wing Monkey,* made in 1923 and released in January 1924.

"Joe the Monk gets a job in the Jungletown street cleaning department. A dog tips over a lion's cage. The wild beasts escape. A frightened nursemaid deserts her charge, but Joe rescues the baby from the lions."

His last film was *Down in Jungle Town.* The synopsis ran: "Joe and some bathing beauties are chased by a lion into a swimming pool. A man, enraged by the unexpected visit of his mother-in-law, runs amuck and shoots up the town. A cop, aided by an elephant, arrests him. Joe sits on a freshly painted bench and is mistaken for an escaped convict. Joe is chased, captured and later released. Then a hungry bear chases a child up a tree. Joe teams with an elephant to rescue the child."

The Universal publicity release on Joe's departure said:

"Joe Martin, famous Universal orang outang comedian, has deserted the screen. He is now the leading Simian attraction of the Al G. Barnes Circus.

"Joe this week bade goodby to the films at Universal City in a last long, lingering farewell. Laura La Plante was present to bid the big man monkey bon voyage. Reginald Denny shook hands with him, and Hoot Gibson gave him a farewell bag of peanuts.

"*Merry-Go-Round* was the last big picture in which he worked. He developed a sudden savage sullenness which made it dangerous for any human actor to work with him. Even Charles B. Murphy, chief trainer, became afraid to handle him."

J. Warren Kerrigan, fresh from *The Covered Wagon* at Paramount, returned to Universal to make *Thundering Dawn* with Anna Q. Nilsson. He played a Bostonian who goes to rot in the tropics. He is followed by Miss Nilsson, his Boston sweetheart. She finds him enmeshed with Winnifred Bryson, whose character the Los Angeles Times, said, "is the Javanese equivalent of the Alaskan dance hall girl, only worse, as immorality is always worse in the tropics." There is a monsoon and a tidal wave that help to wash away Kerrigan's sins and reunite him with Anna Q.

Kerrigan was close to the end of his movie career. In the years just prior to World War I he had been one of the most popular film actors in the world. He was born in Louisville, Kentucky, in 1891. As a child he became stagestruck and carried a copy of Shakespeare's plays around in his pocket. He finally got on the stage where he was spotted by an executive from Essanay while performing in *The Road to Yesterday* in Chicago. From Essanay he spent three years with American Biograph and then went to Universal where his popularity boomed. He began to slip in the early 1920's. Usually a phenomenally successful film gives a career boost to all its major cast members, but *The Covered Wagon* did little for either Kerrigan or Lois Wilson. After *Thundering Dawn,* he went to Vitagraph for *The Man from Bodney's* and *Captain Blood,* but his movie days were numbered. He was the youngest of seven brothers. His twin, Wallace, was born thirty minutes before him.

While it wasn't the best money-maker in 1924 (*The Hunchback* and *Merry-Go-Round* released in 1923 held that position), Universal's best break in 1924 was *Sporting Youth,* which Harry Pollard directed. After leaving *The Leather Pushers* series, Reginald Denny had made two features, *The*

Kentucky Derby and *The Abysmal Brute,* a fight story based on a Jack London novel. They were well received, but did not set the world on fire. *Sporting Youth,* however, established Denny as a top draw and a superb light comedian.

The Byron Morgan story cast Denny as Jimmy Wood, a chauffeur who dreams of becoming a great race driver. His employer sends him on an errand to Del Monte, California, where he is mistaken for "Splinters" Wood, famous English driver, who is supposed to arrive for the race. Despite his protests he is forced to race, but the real "Splinters" Wood shows up. He turns out to be a fugitive with detectives pursuing him. Both Woods become involved, but in the end Jimmy wins the race and the girl.

The picture also started Laura La Plante on her climb to fame as a light comedienne. Denny had seen her around the lot where she had graduated from Century comedies to Hoot Gibson westerns. He thought she had just the spirit of fun needed to complement his own character. Harry Pollard, the

William Desmond and Eileen Sedgwick in the 1924 serial *The Riddle Rider,* based on a story by Arthur B. Reeve.

Reginald Denny, here getting an assist from Laura La Plante in 1925's *Lightning Lover,* was the top Universal male star in the late 1920s.

director, objected, for his wife, Margarita Fischer, was trying to make a comeback. Since the script looked good, Pollard wanted her. Denny won, but he and Pollard never really liked each other thereafter.

On the serial front, Universal scored its biggest hits. William Desmond and Eileen Sedgwick made *The Riddle Rider* from a story by Arthur B. Reeve, who had written *The Exploits of Elaine* for Pearl White. It was the story of a crusading newspaper man who disguises himself to ride through the western oilfields and administer justice where the law has failed. Reeve is said to have drawn his inspiration from Douglas Fairbanks's role in *The Mark of Zorro* in 1920. These early dual identity picture were the spiritual fathers of a long series of similar heroes, ranging from *The Shadow* to *Super-*

The fur pirates have William Duncan trapped in *Wolves of the North,* Duncan's final serial for Universal in 1924. Joe Bonomo is one of the villains.

man. In all of them the hero had a mundane identity, which he stripped off to become the mysterious avenger.

Desmond was born in Dublin, Ireland, in 1881, and came to the United States as a child. He went on the stage and did quite well until he quit to join Triangle in 1916. This was when Harry Aitken of Triangle was bringing in stage stars. Douglas Fairbanks was in the group, along with DeWitt Hopper, Tully Marshall, and others. For several years Desmond played brash juvenile heroes in the manner of the early Fairbanks films and in 1923 moved to Universal to make western features. In westerns his increasing age and growing waistline didn't matter. *The Perils of the Yukon,* with Laura La Plante in 1923, established him as a serial star and *The Riddle Rider* cinched it.

Eileen Sedgwick was born in Galveston, Texas, in 1897. She came from a theatrical family who toured as the "Five Sedgwicks." Her brother Edward, after playing fat heavies in early Century and L–KO comedies, became a director, handling more than twenty Hoot Gibson films in the 1920s. Her sister Josephine (Josie) also worked for Universal.

Other 1924 serial releases included Lucien Albertini, the European strongman, in *The Iron Man,* with "The Hercules of the Screen," Joe Bonomo, as the heavy. Bonomo had doubled for Lon Chaney in the scene in *the Hunchback* where Quasimodo slides down the rope from the Notre Dame bell tower to rescue Esmeralda.

Another Desmond release in this year was *The Ace of Spades,* with former child star Mary

132

McAllister. It was laid against a background of the Oklahoma landrush.

William Duncan closed out his career, which began with Selig, in two final serials, *The Fast Express,* in which he played a railroad detective, and *Wolves of the North,* which dealt with fur thieves in Canada. Joe Bonomo again played a heavy. Edith Johnson was his co-star and Esther Ralston had a good role.

Duncan's removal from the screen was not because of failing popularity. He was growing old and his coordination was getting bad. Edith Johnson, his wife, was alarmed at the risks he took (he rarely employed doubles) and kept pressuring him to quit. Since he had acted as his own director and producer for years, he had plenty of money and didn't need to work.

As director as well as star, Duncan worked out his own stunts. In an interview given close to the end of his career, Duncan explained how he worked out his thrills. In one film the script called for him to pursue the villains in a car and jump a chasm. The location director found one that was thirty-five feet across and ninety feet deep. This was great because an extra camera at the bottom could emphasize the height and add to the apparent danger.

Unfortunately there was no road up the cliff. They had to pull the car up with ropes and manpower. They had to build a bridge across the

Sooner or later all the old-timers seemed to come to Universal. Tom Santschi, a former keystone of the Selig stock company, joined Priscilla Dean in *The Storm Daughter,* a 1924 offering directed by Colin Campbell, another Selig veteran.

Clarence Brown directed *The Signal Tower* in 1924, a railroad story wherein Wallace Beery attacks Rockcliffe Fellowes's wife while the gallant Rocky is trying to save a train. This still shows Beery with Fellowes.

chasm to get the car on the right side. The bridge then had to be removed.

The ground where the car must land sloped back toward the gulf. This meant that when Duncan landed there was the possibility of the car rolling back and plunging over the cliff. A deep cut was made so the car would roll in the opposite direction — if Duncan landed right.

Then on the take-off side, wooden tracks were built on an upward incline. This approach raised the front of the car and permitted it to leap upward as it took off. Brush camouflaged the track.

He made the thirty-five-foot leap satisfactorily, but hit so hard that all four tires burst and he was thrown heavily against the dashboard.

In another scene he wanted a realistic fight. So he told his crew that he had a five dollar gold piece in his pocket and the man who was man enough to get it could have the money. He got a glorious rough and tumble scene, but he said ruefully that

Mary Philbin, Marc McDermott, Rose Dione, and John
Sainpolis in the 1924 film *Rose of Paris.*

Joe Murphy was Andy in the Universal comedies *The
Gumps,* based upon Sidney Smith's famous comic strip.

he never tried that again. The hungry extras really went after the money and he was sore for a week thereafter.

Some other films of 1924 include *The Signal Tower*, with Wallace Beery, Virginia Valli, and Rockcliffe Fellowes, *Rustlers of Montana* with Jack Hoxie, *The Family Secret* with Baby Peggy,

Baby Peggy Montgomery, the prototype of Shirley Temple, with Edward Earle in *The Family Secret*, 1924.

Mary Philbin in *Fools' Highway*, and *The Storm Daughter* with Priscilla Dean nearing the end of her career. Tom Santschi, a Selig stalwart for years, co-starred with her. Mary Philbin also starred in *Rose of Paris*.

In the comedy field Universal had definitely lost its top position. Neely Edward and Bert Roach had replaced the Lee Moran-Eddie Lyons team. Sam Van Ronkel Productions were releasing a series with Joe Murphy based upon *The Gumps*, the Sidney Smith cartoon strip. Buddy Messenger, Wanda Wiley, Arthur Trimble as *Buster Brown*, and Eddie Gordon were with Century Comedies.

Profits had fallen so badly that Laemmle shook up his sales staff. Al Lichtman was brought in from Preferred as general sales manager. Lichtman kicked off the 1924 sales meeting by telling the convention: "I have come to the conclusion that exhibitors want bigger pictures, and will pay to get them, because they make more money with them. This is thoroughly borne out by the experience of Jewel pictures. So I am going to propose to Mr. Laemmle that he give us thirty-six Jewels for the next season."

Jewel was the trademark under which Big U

marketed its better and more expensive pictures. Laemmle told the convention: "I have decided to carry out the entire program which Mr. Lichtman has outlined. It will be very costly. I have roughly outlined it in my mind. It doesn't seem to me that it can be carried out without an expenditure of five-million-dollars more than we have ever put into a production program in the history of Universal."

This meant simply that Big U intended to challenge the feature makers on their own ground. Paramount's *Covered Wagon*, *The Ten Commandments*, and Universal's own *The Hunchback of Notre Dame* and *Merry-Go-Round* had shown unmistakably that big pictures meant big profits. Therefore, Laemmle said, he was justified in

Herbert Rawlinson, whose *Damon and Pythias* was the first film shot at Universal City in 1915, made *Stolen Secrets* in 1924. He played Miles Manning, a criminologist who put on a disguise to infiltrate a criminal gang.

announcing thirty-six Jewel features for the next year. Bernard McConville was appointed supervisor to oversee Jewel productions. An announcement

135

Rupert Julian, center holding surveyor's marker, checks plans with Llewelynn Steel Company engineers as mule teams in the background break ground for the famous Paris Opera House set used in *The Phantom of the Opera*. Exterior of the set is shown at the top of the hill. Picture taken in 1924. The film was released the following year and became an all-time classic of the screen.

from the publicity department said that McConville was going to New York to buy stories for the 1925 season.

Unfortunately, the Jewels released in 1924 and 1925 did not have the stars or the stories necessary to carry out the big plans of Lichtman and Laemmle. The huge outlay of money—huge for the time—required Laemmle and Cochrane to sell stock to the public to raise the capital. Only one picture made lived up to its promise as a critical and financial blockbuster. This was *The Phantom of*

the Opera, which with *The Hunchback*, make the two best-known of all Big U's silent films.

The *Phantom* is from a gothic-type novel by Gaston Leroux. The story is about a hideous musician who hides behind a mask and lives a tortured life in the cellers of the Paris Opera House. He kidnaps Mary Philbin and she tears the mask from his face, disclosing a horrible vision to the audience. In the final reel the Phantom is chased through the streets of Paris by a vengeful mob.

Norman Kerry, Mary Philbin, and Arthur Edmund Carewe in *The Phantom of the Opera.* They all gave excellent performances, but were overshadowed by Chaney's *tour de force.*

Rupert Julian was the enthusiasm behind the project. It was okayed by Laemmle after Irving Thalberg and Louis B. Mayer agreed to loan Lon Chaney for the role. Chaney had been given a long term contract with the new Metro-Goldwyn company on Thalberg's insistence. His first M–G film *He Who Gets Slapped,* had been a hit.

Lous B. Mayer, who had little use for Laemmle, was reluctant to make the loan. Thalberg insisted. He said that a hit—and he was sure that the *Phantom* would be a hit—would enhance Chaney's value to Metro–Goldwyn.

Julian, influenced by Von Stroheim whom he admired, shoveled money into the film. He also proved quite temperamental, quarreling with every-

one from McConville to Chaney. Chaney, who was striving for more naturalism, objected to some of the theatrical posturing Julian wanted. In the end Edward Sedgwick was brought in to reshoot the chase ending and supervise the cutting. He was credited along with Julian in the advertising, which further enraged Julian who soon left Big U to join Cecil B. DeMille at Producers Distributing Corporation.

Chaney's makeup as The Phantom was among his masterpieces. Yet it was basically simple. He built up a high forehead, upturned his nose by inserting bent wires in the nostrils and wore hideous false teeth. His horrible face was not revealed in advance publicity. This created an

137

Lon Chaney as "The Red Death" in the masked ball scene
in *The Phantom of the Opera*.

Originally announced as *The Clash*, this Percy Marmont-
Alma Rubens film reached the screen as *A Woman's Faith*.
Edward Laemmle directed.

Workmen from the Llewelyn Steel Company rush the framework for the opera house set for the *Phantom of the Opera,* released in 1925.

audience shock effect when Mary Philbin first rips the mask away to reveal Eric's face in one of the most terrifying scenes in movie history.

Chaney claimed in a *Colliers* interview that he never used masks, *"not even in The Phantom of the Opera."* This is not true. A close examination of stills of Chaney as the Red Death, a skeleton-faced personification of Death, definitely shows a death's head mask.

Universal quoted Laemmle in publicity releases as saying that *The Phantom of the Opera* was his greatest achievement. They claimed that fifty principal players were used with over five-thousand extras.

> Construction of the exact reproduction of the famous Paris Opera House marks the ultimate in motion picture settings. No studio in the world is large enough to hold this setting; a special building had to be put up for it. The completed setting could easily contain the two largest stages in Hollywood.
> The interior of the opera house is over 100 feet high, containing five tiers of balconies, and seating 3,000 people. The stage is 100 feet wide and 75 feet high, exactly the dimensions of the original.
> The grand staircase, one hundred feet high, with six levels, was built in exact size. In this setting, the famous sculptures and decorations are exact reproductions of the originals.

Such superlatives were not out of place. As a permanent set, the opera house paid for itself in future films and in rental to other companies.

Norman Kerry and Mary Philbin handled the romantic interest in the film, but all attention was on Chaney. Although he is best known for his MGM features, the three greatest roles of Lon Chaney's career were *The Hunchback of Notre Dame, The Phantom of the Opera,* and *Tell It to the Marines.* Two of these three were made by Universal.

Norman Kerry was second only to Reginald Denny as Big U's most popular male lead (excluding westerns) in the last half of the 1920s. Kerry was born in Rochester, New York, and first had the Navy as a career objective. He received an appointment to the Naval Academy at Annapolis in 1910, but turned it down at the last minute. He tried college, but was bored by that. He then joined his father, who dealt in cattle and hides.

While on a trip to Argentina to buy beef, he met Art Acord, who was touring South America with a Wild West troupe. Returning to the U.S., Kerry joined the army in 1917 and was a lieutenant in World War I. After the war he became a traveling salesman, which took him to Southern Californa. Here he met Art Acord again and the cowboy actor introduced Kerry to films. After working for Brunton and Allan Dwan, he was signed by Universal. He continued to work for Big U, except for a break with Metro-Goldwyn, for the rest of the silent era.

For the 1925—26 season, Universal's star roster had shrunk to Reginald Denny, Laura La Plante, Virginia Valli, Hoot Gibson, Norman Kerry, House Peters, Pat O'Malley, Glenn Hunter, Constance Bennett (just beginning her career), George Sidney, Jacqueline Logan, Jack Pickford, Jean Hersholt, Eugene O'Brien, and Mary Philbin.

Hoot was in the list because his pictures were so successful that he was advanced from the B group to Jewel release.

Not one person in this roster of actors and actresses could possibly compete with such names from other studios as Gloria Swanson, Pola Negri, Douglas Fairbanks, Mary Pickford, Rudolph Valentino, Bebe Daniels, Richard Dix, and others of their caliber.

Laemmle's failure to put his money into a theater chain and top stars was slowly backing Universal against the wall.

12 Noises in the Background

For the 1925-26 season Universal promised exhibitors thirty great Jewel pictures and twenty-four Blue Streak westerns for a total of fifty-four features. In addition they promised six serials and 104 comedies.

The thirty Jewels, most of which were glass instead of gems, were in the order of their release:

Reginald Denny in *California Straight Ahead* with Gertrude Olmstead and directed by Harry Pollard. An enjoyable Byron Morgan racing story of a young man who crosses the country in a special house trailer, rescues the girl from being stranded in the desert, and then wins a big auto race in the last reel.

Rex Beach's *The Goose Woman,* directed by Clarence Brown with Jack Pickford, Louise Dresser, and Constance Bennett. Based by Beach on an incident in the famed Halls-Mills trial, the story involved a former opera star who now raises geese. Her hunger for publicity in a murder case causes her to involve her son in a murder accusation. The picture was a critical success and added luster to Brown's name, but the public was not overly interested in goose women.

Hoot Gibson in *Spook Ranch* with Helen Ferguson. A typical Gibson western and his first under the Jewel banner.

Virginia Valli and Eugene O'Brien in *Siege* with Mary Alden as the tyrant mother. Virginia marries Eugene and moves into a house dominated by his mother. It was directed by Sven Gade.

Norman Kerry and Patsy Ruth Miller in *Beauty and the Beast.*

Laura La Plante in *The Teaser* with Pat O'Malley.

House Peters in *The Storm Breaker* with Ruth Clifford.

Reginald Denny in *Where Was I?* This was an amusing story of a young man who is accused by a girl he never saw before of promising to marry her on March 15. He, in turn, has no recollection at all of what he did on that day. William A. Seiter directed.

Hoot Gibson in *The Arizona Sweepstakes* with Helen Lynch.

The Home Maker, a King Baggott production with Alice Joyce and Clive Brook.

Glenn Hunter in *The Little Giant.* Hunter was a hit in both the stage and screen versions of *Merton of the Movies,* but was never able to repeat his success and certainly not in this poor release.

Laura La Plante in *The Beautiful Cheat,* a society comedy set in Long Island.

Mary Philbin in *Stella Maris,* a remake of an old Mary Pickford story, in which Philbin plays both the slave and the crippled girl she must serve.

My Old Dutch with May McAvoy and Jean Hersholt.

Hoot Gibson in *The Man in the Saddle* with Fay Wray.

Reginald Denny in *The Whole Town's Talking.*

Norman Kerry in *On the Frontier.*

The Universal back lot looked like this in 1925. Tents in the foreground are for the Joe Bonomo serial *The Great Circus Mystery*.

Jacqueline Logan and Cullen Landis in *Peacock Feathers*.

Two Blocks Away with George Sidney and Charlie Murray in a Jewish-Irish comedy that is notable mainly because it led to the *Cohens and Kellys* series that made a lot of money for Universal.

Hoot Gibson in *Kings Up,* House Peters in *The Man from Outside,* Mary Philbin in *Sally in Our Alley,* Reginald Denny in *This Way Out,* and *The Love Thrill.*

Then Hoot again in *Chip of the Flying U* from the novel by B. M. Bowers. Although it lacked a lot of the bang-bang action of most of Gibson's pictures, it was his greatest single hit. Dr. Della

Whitmore is the sister of the ranch owner where Chip is foreman. He fakes an injury so she will treat him and he can be near her. He is making progress when she discovers his subterfuge. After some sparring, he kidnaps her and she discovers that she is in love with him after all.

Norman Kerry in *Under Western Skies, The Still Alarm,* and *Sporting Life* with all-star casts, *His People* with Rudolph Schildkraut, and Hoot again in *The Calgary Stampede.* This was filmed at the Calgary rodeo and Hoot proved he had not forgotten his early training by winning the chariot race.

The Blue Streak westerns were divided in eight films each by three stars. Art Acord had *Sky High*

By 1925 former child star Mary McAlister was playing romantic leads. Here she is with William Desmond in *The Ace of Spades*, a serial based on the Oklahoma landrush.

Josie Sedgwick made a determined cowgirl in *Daring Days,* filmed in 1925. Her brother Edward was a Universal director and her sister Eileen was a serial queen. Their father also had a job with the company.

heavy, came into his own as a hero, making *The Great Circus Mystery* for release in March 1925 and *Perils of the Wild,* based upon the *Swiss Family Robinson* novel, for August release. *Perils of the Wild* was directed by Francis Ford, marking his short return to Universal.

Ford also directed William Desmond in *The Winking Idol,* a serial released in early 1926. His old co-star, Grace Cunard, continued to play supporting roles at Big U. She was in the serial *Fighting With Buffalo Bill,* directed by Ray Taylor, which was released in the 1926-27 season. They never again showed any professional interest in each other after they broke their original partnership.

The 1926-27 season was a repeat of the previous season. Westerns and serials were the company's best money makers, but they were not exceptionally profitable because they did not play the big houses. They were primarily Saturday matinee stuff. The same audience that whooped

Corral and seven others. Among Jack Hoxie's eight was "the big special Western novelty, *The White Outlaw* with SCOUT, the equine marvel, and BUNK, the canine sensation."

The final eight were divided between various B western stars, including Josie Sedgwick who made *Daring Days.*

Arthur Lake, the future Dagwood, made a comedy a week for Bluebird, as did Charles Puffy, an Arbuckle type of fat man. Fred Humes, Ed Cobb, and Jack Mower divided fifty-two two-reel action western shorts among themselves. These, with 105 (two a week) newsreels, made Universal schedule 314 separate releases for the 1925-26 season.

On the serial front, Joe Bonomo, after years as a

Prowlers of the Night was a 1926 Blue Streak western with Barbara Kent and Fred Humes.

Strongman Joe Bonomo and mystery man Slim Cole in *The Great Circus Mystery*, a 1925 serial.

and hollered on Saturday did not fill the theaters during the week.

This was shown in a very successful series called the *Collegians*. Nineteen-year-old Carl Laemmle, Jr., was given the production responsibility. The series was a sort of updated Frank Merrill with George Lewis as the college hero, Eddie Phillips was a not-so-heavy heavy, and Churchill Ross was the sissified comic relief. Hayden Stevenson, the fight manager from *The Leather Pushers,* was the wise coach. The success of this series inspired Universal to push the cast into a feature, *The Flourflusher,* released in 1928. Marion Nixon took the place of Dorothy Gulliver, otherwise the cast was intact. As a feature, the college idea was too weak to sustain interest.

Some pictures that did hit the public fancy in

the 1926-27 season were *A Cheerful Fraud,* wherein a rich man (Reginald Denny) takes a menial job in order to woo a social secretary (Gertrude Olmstead); Laura La Plante in *The Midnight Sun,* the story of a Russian dancer directed by Dmitri Buchowetski; and House Peters and Virginia Valli in *Prisoners of the Storm.* In the latter, Peters, accused of murder, is trapped in a cabin by a snowslide along with the man pursuing him, a crooked doctor who is the real killer, and the girl (Virginia Valli) who is the daughter of the man Peters supposedly killed.

In 1927 Hayden Stevenson, after years of supporting roles, got his chance to be a hero as *Blake of Scotland Yard,* which also had Grace Cunard in a supporting role.

Edward Everett Horton had an amusing light

144

Robert E. Homans, Elsie Benham, and Cuyler Suplee in
Fighting With Buffalo Bill, 1926.

Hoot Gibson had Kathleen Key as love support in the 1927
film *Hey, Hey, Cowboy*. Edward Laemmle directed.

The Collegians was a popular Universal Series in 1927. Westlake Park in Los Angeles (later renamed MacArthur Park) was the setting for this boat race scene.

The *Collegians* series was so popular that Universal starred the cast in the feature *The Fourflusher* in 1928. From left are Eddie Phillips, Marion Nixon, Churchill Ross, and George Lewis.

Fifth Avenue Models in 1925 reunited the lovers of *The Phantom of the Opera*, Norman Kerry and Mary Philbin, but not as successfully as in the previous film.

comedy role in *Taxi! Taxi!* with Marion Nixon, Burr MacIntosh, and Lucien Littlefield. He played a young architect who has to buy a taxi to get his girl home.

The returns on *The Phantom of the Opera,* despite its over a million cost, were good enough to encourage Laemmle to risk another big picture. This was *Uncle Tom's Cabin,* the venerable standby of traveling stock shows since the Civil War. When the question came up about its creaking age, Harry Pollard, who wanted to make it, pointed to *Way Down East,* which Griffith had made with great success.

Pollard cast his wife, Margarita Fischer, as Eliza, George Seligman as Simon Legree, Virginia Grey as Little Eva, and James B. Lowe as Uncle Tom. Mona Ray, a nineteen-year vaudeville actress, wanted the Topsy role, but Pollard wouldn't even see her. He thought her too old, even though Mary Pickford was still playing children at thirty. Mona, who was only four-foot- seven inches in height, was

as determined as she was small. She heard Pollard was to attend a premiere at one of Sid Grauman's theaters. Grauman always had a stage prologue before each film. Mona offered to work in it for nothing if she could appear in blackface. Grauman demurred, for his prologues were supposed to be in the spirit of the films they preceded. She told him what she had in mind. Sid, who loved a joke more than money or art, agreed.

In the middle of her act, Mona walked to the edge of the stage, put her hands on her hips and spoke directly at Pollard in the audience: "I wasn't born! I just growed!" The bewildered audience didn't know what she meant, but Pollard did. It was one of Topsy's lines from *Uncle Tom's Cabin.*

She got the part.

The highlight, of course, was Eliza crossing the ice, pursued by Simon Legree's bloodhounds. Today's movie historians are silent on this scene while they enthuse about Lillian Gish on the ice in Griffith's *Way Down East,* but the writer of this book, recalling the film through the eyes of a ten-year-old, thought it very thrilling indeed. Unfortunately, it was too old-fashioned for the flappers and sheiks of 1927. They preferred pictures like *Painting the Town* with Glenn Tryon and Patsy Ruth Miller with its wild party scenes, which Universal released that same year. *Silk Stockings* with Laura La Plante packed them in also.

But the best remembered film of 1927 was Miss

A stunt man with a doll doubles for Margarita Fischer a Lassie Lou Aherne in the 1927 version of *Uncle Ton's Cabin,* directed by Harry Pollard.

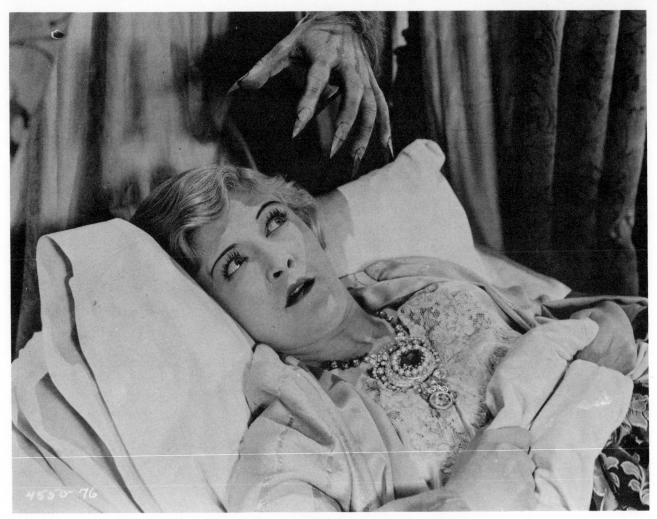

Paul Leni, as director, made an atmospheric wonder of *The Cat and the Canary,* in which Laura LaPlante, wearing the necklace she has just inherited, is menaced by a strange hand from a secret wall panel.

La Plante's *The Cat and the Canary,* directed by German import, Paul Leni. It is the story of a young girl called to a mysterious house for the reading of a will. She inherits a beautiful necklace, that she — for some odd reason—wears to bed. The house is filled with strange people who thought they should have inherited instead of Laura. She in turn is protected by Creighton Hale, who loves her.

The story, with its sliding door and mysterious doings, is laughable today, but when I saw it in 1927 it thrilled audiences as much as *Dracula* did in a later day.

The problems of 1926, '27, and '28 were complicated by noises in the background made by a man in blackface singing "Mammy". Laemmle was violently opposed to sound films, and for good reason. Back in the days when he was in the forefront of motion pciture pioneering, he had taken a flyer in sound films. Through the years there had been several attempts to add sound to film, beginning with Thomas A. Edison's project. Unfortunately these systems depended upon synchronizing phonograph records with the screen and none of the early ones worked satisfactorily.

Laemmle was not the only one who resisted going to sound, but all were forced to do so because the near-bankrupt Warner Brothers were forcing the issue. Universal continued to drag its feet on the conversion to sound.

As a result 1928 was a poor year for the

company. The biggest hit again was a serial. Actually Big U released five serials this year, including two by old reliable William Desmond. They were patterned after his successful *The Riddle Rider* of 1924. One was called *The Mystery Rider* and the other was called *The Vanishing Rider*. But the big hit was *Tarzan the Mighty*, released in August 1928. Frank Merrill, who had once doubled for Elmo Lincoln as Tarzan, had the lead. Natalie Kingston played Mary Trevor, instead of the traditional Jane.

In the story Mary and her brother, Bobby (Bobby Nelson, son of director Jack Nelson), are shipwrecked on the African coast where they are aided by Tarzan. Tarzan is opposed by Black John (Al Ferguson), a descendent of pirates, who now rules an African village.

Tarzan, who is actually the son of Lord Greystoke, a British nobleman, and his wife, who perished in the jungle after their child was born, is being sought by his English relatives. His uncle, Lorimer Johnston, arrives in Africa seeking the child of his dead brother. Black John learns of this. He shoots a vine in two that Tarzan is swinging upon. The apeman falls and is knocked unconscious. Black John thinks him dead and steals papers and photographs left by the dead Lord Greystoke. He shows these to Tarzan's uncle and is accepted as the real Lord Greystoke.

Black John is exposed, but attempts to kill both

William Desmond proves a hardy fighter in the 1928 serial
The Mystery Rider.

151

William Desmond learns from Frank Rice that the bad guys went thataway in the 1928 chapter play *The Vanishing Rider*.

While this still gives the impression of a burlesque comedy, *The Haunted Island*, 1928, with Jack Daugherty and Helen Foster, was supposed to be high adventure about a search for buried treasure. Robert F. Hill directed.

Tarzan and his uncle so he can go to England and claim Tarzan's heritage. After considerable difficulty Tarzan, with the help of Tantor the elephant, overcomes his enemy. He then refuses to return to England and take the title, claiming he

Bobby Nelson, Al Ferguson, and Natalie Kingston in *Tarzan the Mighty,* the 1928 Universal serial starring Frank Merrill.

was born in the jungle and that was where he belongs. Mary declares she will remain with him.

Merrill was a man of tremendous physique and made a superb Tarzan. A champion gymnast and acrobat, he was more at home in the trees than any other Tarzan before or since. However, the writers cheated on occasion. I have a distinct recollection of one chapter ending with a lion's springing at Tarzan. The next week, when I returned breathless to see how Tarzan fought off the lion, the lion did not spring at all. He only shook his head and turned away.

The following year Universal released a sequel, *Tarzan the Tiger,* which had sound effects and a small amount of dialogue so it could be advertised as "Part Talking." It was also recut as a silent pciture, titled and exhibited in those houses not yet wired for sound.

The big picture for 1929 was *Showboat,* based on the book by Edna Ferber and the musical by Jerome Kern and Oscar Hammerstein II. It was the story of Magnolia Ravenal (Laura La Plante) who grew up on a showboat on the Mississippi River, piloted by her father, Captain Andy Hawks (Otis

Harlan), and presided over by her prim and grim mother, Parthy Ann (Emily Fitzroy). When they lose a leading man because Parthy Ann objects to the character of a girl Julie (Alma Rubens) and the leading man goes with the girl, Captain Andy hires a gamble, Gaylord Ravenal, to take his place.

Suspicious Parthy Ann watches Ravenal and her daughter, but he makes love to Magnolia in whispers as they play their roles on stage. Parthy Ann predicts dire fate for her daughter when Magnolia, without permission, marries Ravenal. They go to Chicago where they live like a king and queen one month and in the dumps the next as his gambling fortune rises and falls.

Frank Merrill starred in two Tarzan serials for Universal after Joe Bonomo, the first choice, dropped out. This shows Merrill in *Tarzan the Tiger,* a ten-chapter serial released in 1929. It had sound effects and is famous in Tarzan history as the first time the "bull ape cry of victory" was recorded.

In the meantime, Captain Andy is swept overboard and drowned during a storm on the river. Parthy Ann, who always professed to hate the

Laura La Plante strummed her banjo well enough, but her minstrel songs were sung by a woman behind the black curtain because the fledgling sound film industry had not yet learned to dub in voices for nonsinging actresses. The picture is *Show Boat*, 1929.

Even the smallest theaters were wiring for sound. The days of the silent film were over. Al Jolson in *Sonny Boy* for Warners, *Broadway Melody* for MGM, *Fox Movietone Follies of 1929*, *Paramount on Parade*, and others were raking in money while far better silents were dying at the box office.

Laemmle stopped his objection. Convert to all-talking pictures and damn the expense. While his subordinates cheered this decision, they shuddered at his next. He announced that he was appointing twenty-year-old Carl Laemmle, Jr., as chief of production. When objections were raised about the young man's youth, Laemmle said, "Look at Thalberg."

At the sales convention that year Laemmle laid it on the line. He said frankly that 1928 and 1929 had been bad financial years for the company. "I am not going to say anymore on the subject, because if I do you will see a few tears . . . . We want to sell to everybody, but we have to have the

showboat, carries on the show. A daughter is born to the Ravenals. Then when fortune deserts Ravenal for a long time, Magnolia earns her living singing with a banjo songs she learned on the showboat. After Parthy Ann dies, Magnolia goes back to the showboat. And at the end a gray-haired Ravenal comes back to her.

Ravenal was played by Joseph Schildkraut, son of Rudolph Schildkraut. The picture was directed by Harry Pollard and was a beauty to behold.

The film was part talking only, but all the wonderful songs from the musical stage production were recorded: *Old Man River, Make Believe,* and *Can't Help Lovin' That Man.* In addition there were Negro folk songs sung by a voice double for Laura La Plante. Sound dubbing was not possible at that time. Miss La Plante performed in front of a curtain, mouthing the words as a singer and banjo player behind the screen recorded into the microphone. A silent version with subtitles was also distributed, but it lost considerably in not having the music.

Paul Fejos, director, joins his star and producer, Myrna Kennedy and Carl Laemmle, Jr., on the way to the *Broadway* set.

houses that can pay the most money first. If we can't get them, we might just as well quit now. In other words, get every last dollar the law allows, and then some."

Meanwhile back in Universal City, Carl Laemmle, Jr., was working on production problems for *Broadway,* the company's first all-talking picture. Henry McRae, who had been with Big U from its organization, was telling Laemmle that he could lick the sound problem if he got permission to start an all-talking serial. Plans were being pushed to drop all silents, even silent versions of talking pictures.

The curtain had fallen on the silent years of Universal.

Afterword

The silent era at Universal spanned seventeen years, from 1912 to 1929. It was a time of trouble and turmoil in the industry. In the beginning—from 1912 to about 1917, Big U played a dramatic and often decisve role in the industry. D. W. Griffith has been credited with making the industry an art, and all the credit he has received is due him. However, it must be remembered that Griffith worked for men who were dedicated to maintaining the status quo in the industry. Griffith could experiment and innovate only within the confines of his two-reels.

Expansion beyond that, which resulted eventually in *The Birth of a Nation,* was possible only because the independents— of whom Carl Laemmle was the leader—forcibly broke the motion picture trust and eased the restraints on artistic expression.

Laemmle brought integrity into the chaotic exchange system. He made the store theater into a family theater for the first time. He created the star system by his Lawrence-Pickford raids on Biograph. He gave a surprising number of later famous names their initial chance. And for five years his pictures were among the most popular in America. After that there was a gradual decline until the company under Laemmle hit bottom in 1928 and 1929.

Laemmle expressed his confidence in the future. Looking at Junior, whom Uncle Carl had entrusted with production, observers in and out of the company shook their heads sadly.

So what did Junior do? He produced *Broadway.* A hit. The next year he produced Lewis Milestone's *All Quiet on the Western Front.* An Academy Award winner and still a classic. Just down the short years were *Dracula* and *Frankenstein.*

Uncle Carl sold his interests in 1936, bowing out at sixty-nine, but Universal went on. Deanna Durbin became the breadwinner. James Stewart and Marlene Dietrich made *Destry Rides Again.* And so on until today when Big U remains the last of the major studios that functions as a studio.

Since the inauguration of the Universal Studio Tours, thousands flock to Universal City each year — as Uncle Carl put it sixty years ago when he first invited the public in—"to see how movies are made."

Surely if Uncle Carl—wherever his spirit may be—can see his old studio today, he must be saying, "I told you so!"

Index of Universal Films

This index includes only the IMP and Universal films listed in this book. Release dates may vary because many of these films were sold on States Rights and release dates coincided with the buyer's schedules.

Index of Names

Ray, Mona, 149
Razeto, Stella, 81
Reardon, Ned, 81
Reeve, Arthur B., 131
Reid, Wallace, 65, 66, 96
Rhodes, Billie, 81
Rice, Frank, 152
Rich, Irene, 116, 121
Ritchie, Billie, 31, 51, 81
Ritchie, Franklin, 81
Roach, Bert, 136
Robbins, Mark, 83
Roberts, Edith, 83
Ross, Churchill, 146
Rosselli, Rex, 83, 115
Rubens, Alma, 8, 138, 153
Russell, William, 58

Sabatini, Rafael, 85, 87
Sainpolis, John, 34
Salisbury, Monroe, 92
Salter, Harry, 26
Santschi, Paul (Tom), 36, 133, 135
Scharrer, Jack 81
Schildkraut, Joseph, 154
Schildkraut, Rudolph, 141, 154
Scott, Cyril, 57
Sedgwich, Edward, 103, 104, 119, 125, 132, 137
Sedgwick, Eileen, 103, 119, 131, 132
Sedgwick, Josephine (Josie), 103, 119, 132, 143
Seiter, William A., 8, 117, 118, 140
Selbie, Evelyn, 93
Selig, Col. William, 13
Seligman, George, 149
Sennett, Mack, 12, 14, 15, 91, 92
Sheehan, Perley Poore, 87, 120, 122, 123
Shelby, Gertrude, 83
Shields, Ernest, 38, 83
Short, Antrim, 81, 84
Shubert Brothers, 35
Shumm, Harry, 36, 37, 48, 49
Sidney, George, 139, 141
Sills, Milton, 125

Sisson, Vera, 63-64
Sloman, Edward, 8, 39, 48
Smalley, Phillips, 39, 40, 42, 54, 63, 65, 70, 83, 86
Smiley, Joe, 25
Smith, Frank A., 83
Stanley, Forrest, 123, 125
Stanton, Richard, 83
Steiner, William, 16
Sterling, Ford, 14, 15, 30
Sterling, Richard, 83
Stern, Julius, 61
Stevenson, Hayden, 117, 118, 144, 148
Stewart, Roy, 91, 128
Stonehouse, Ruth, 89
Stone, Lewis, 8
Stowell, William, 39, 77, 79, 93
Suplee, Cuyler, 145
Swain, Mack, 91
Swanson, Bill, 13, 15-16, 19-20, 28, 29, 46
Swanson, Gloria, 109

Taft, President William H., 29
Taylor, Estelle, 123, 125
Taylor, Ray, 143
Tempest, Marie, 57
Thalberg, Irving, 83, 104, 106, 107, 108, 119, 120, 122, 137
Theby, Rosemary, 39, 83, 96
Thomas, Bob, 34
Thompson, Fred, 125, 127
Thornby, Robert T., 121, 122
Thornton, Elsie, 95
Torrence, Ernest, 122
Tourneur, Maurice, 8
Trimble, Arthur, 135
Tryon, Glen, 149
Tucker, George Loane, 26, 35, 36, 113
Turner, Otis, 54, 63

Valentino, Rudolph, 99, 100, 101, 129
Valli, Virginia, 119, 120, 121, 135, 140, 144
Vance, Louis Joseph, 32, 39, 96
Vernon, Agnes, 83

Vokes, Harry, 57
Von Stroheim, Eric, 7, 83, 104, 105, 106, 107, 119, 120
Voss, Fatty, 83

Walcamp, Marie, 83, 89, 91, 100-102, 103
Wallack, H. H., 83
Walsh, Blanch, 57
Walsh, George, 125
Walthal, Henry B. 92, 96
Walton, Gladys, 109, 113, 115
Ward, Hap, 57
Ware, Helen, 57, 81
Warner Brothers, 156
Warren, E. A., 112
Warrenton, Lule, 83
Weber, Lois, 39, 40, 42, 54, 65, 70, 83, 86, 91
Welch, William, 83, 115
Westover, Winifred, 104
White, Glen, 83
White, Pearl, 8, 80
Wierman, Marie, 62
Willard, Jess, 61, 62
Willatt, Doc, 26
Williams, Kathlyn, 36
Williamson Brothers, 88-89
Wilson, Al, 127
Wilson, Ben, 31, 32, 50, 83, 87, 91
Wilson, Elsie Jane, 67, 83, 85, 86
Wilson, John Fleming, 40
Wilson, Lois, 8, 81, 83, 96, 130
Wilson, Roberta, 87
Windsor, Claire, 130
Witwer, H. C., 118
Worne, Duke, 95
Woodrow, Mrs. Wilson, 75
Woods, Dorothy, 125, 126
Worsley, Wallace, 7, 121, 122
Worthington, William, 46, 48, 54, 55, 83

Zukor, Adolph, 33, 46, 65, 80, 100, 129